Free Video

Free Video

Essential Test Tips Video from Trivium Test Prep

Dear Customer,

Thank you for purchasing from Trivium Test Prep! We're honored to help you prepare for your CLEP exam.

To show our appreciation, we're offering a **FREE *CLEP Essential Test Tips* Video by Trivium Test Prep.*** Our video includes 35 test preparation strategies that will make you successful on the CLEP. All we ask is that you email us your feedback and describe your experience with our product. Amazing, awful, or just so-so: we want to hear what you have to say!

To receive your **FREE *CLEP Essential Test Tips* Video**, please email us at 5star@triviumtestprep.com. Include "Free 5 Star" in the subject line and the following information in your email:

1. The title of the product you purchased.
2. Your rating from 1 – 5 (with 5 being the best).
3. Your feedback about the product, including how our materials helped you meet your goals and ways in which we can improve our products.
4. Your full name and shipping address so we can send your **FREE *CLEP Essential Test Tips* Video**.

If you have any questions or concerns please feel free to contact us directly at 5star@triviumtestprep.com.

Thank you!

– Trivium Test Prep Team

*To get access to the free video please email us at 5star@triviumtestprep.com, and please follow the instructions above.

CLEP College Mathematics Study Guide 2021-2022

Comprehensive Review with Practice Test Questions for the CLEP College Math Exam

Printed in the United States of America.

Table of Contents

Online Resources

To help you fully prepare for your CLEP College Mathematics exam, Accepted includes online resources with the purchase of this study guide.

PRACTICE TEST

In addition to the practice test included in this book, we also offer an online exam. Since many exams today are computer based, getting to practice your test-taking skills on the computer is a great way to prepare.

FLASH CARDS

A convenient supplement to this study guide, Accepted's flash cards enable you to review important terms easily on your computer or smartphone.

CHEAT SHEETS

Review the core skills you need to master the exam with easy-to-read Cheat Sheets.

FROM STRESS to SUCCESS

Watch From Stress to Success, a brief but insightful YouTube video that offers the tips, tricks, and secrets experts use to score higher on the exam.

REVIEWS

Leave a review, send us helpful feedback, or sign up for Accepted promotions—including free books!

Access these materials at: **http://www.acceptedinc.com/clep-college-math-online-resources**.

Introduction

Congratulations on choosing to take the CLEP College Mathematics exam! By purchasing this book, you've taken an important step on your path to college.

This guide will provide you with a detailed overview of the CLEP College Mathematics exam so that you know exactly what to expect on test day. We'll take you through all the concepts covered on the exam and give you the opportunity to test your knowledge with practice questions. Even if it's been a while since you last took a major test, don't worry; we'll make sure you're more than ready!

What is the CLEP?

The College-Level Examination Program, or CLEP, offers standardized tests in thirty-three subjects. The CLEP assesses college-level knowledge and allows students to demonstrate that they have proficiency in a subject so that they may bypass the coursework. If a student passes the exam, he or she earns college credit without having to take a single class. Anyone can take the CLEP, but it is designed specifically for people who have had experiences that have allowed them to obtain substantial expertise outside of the classroom. This includes students who have been homeschooled or undertaken extensive independent study, students who studied outside of the United States, adults returning to school after being the workforce, and members of the military.

Approximately 2,900 colleges and universities in the United States grant CLEP credit. Each college or university determines which exams it will accept and sets its own passing score for each exam. Typically, these range from fifty to sixty out of eighty points. Each college also decides how much credit an exam is worth. Colleges will usually offer three credits for an exam, but some schools offer more (depending on the test), and some may offer only an exemption from the requirement but no credit toward graduation. If credits are given, they are added to your transcript just like credits from your coursework would be. CLEP credits carry the same weight as any other earned credits.

What's on the CLEP College Mathematics Exam?

The CLEP College Mathematics exam gauges college-level content knowledge equivalent to a single-semester college math course for students who are not majoring in mathematics or in fields not requiring an advanced knowledge of mathematics. Test questions are divided into two types: half of the questions will ask you to solve routine math problems, while the other half will ask you to demonstrate your mastery of mathematical concepts by solving nonroutine problems. Candidates are expected to demonstrate thorough conceptual knowledge in a range of topics, including algebra and functions, counting and probability, data analysis and statistics, financial mathematics, geometry, logic and sets, and numbers.

You will have ninety minutes to answer approximately sixty multiple-choice questions, including unscored pretest questions.

What's on the CLEP College Mathematics Exam?

Content Area	Topics	Percentage of Exam
Algebra and Functions	▶ Equations, linear equalities, systems of linear equations ▶ Interpretation, representation, and evaluation of functions ▶ Graphs of functions ▶ Linear and exponential growth ▶ Applications	20%
Counting and Probability	▶ Multiplication rule, combinations, and permutations ▶ Core concepts in probability ▶ Applications	10%
Data Analysis and Statistics	▶ Data interpretation and representation ▶ Numerical summaries of data ▶ Standard deviation and normal distribution ▶ Applications	15%
Financial Mathematics	▶ Percents ▶ Interest ▶ Present value and future value ▶ Applications	20%
Geometry	▶ Triangles and quadrilaterals ▶ Parallel and perpendicular lines ▶ Circles ▶ Applications	10%

Content Area	Topics	Percentage of Exam
Logic and Sets	▶ Logical operations and statements ▶ Set relationships ▶ Operations on sets ▶ Applications	15%
Numbers	▶ Properties of numbers and their operations ▶ Elementary number theory ▶ Measurement ▶ Absolute value ▶ Applications	10%

Test-takers are expected to demonstrate mastery of core algebraic concepts. You will be asked to use analytic and graphical methods to solve equations, linear inequalities, and systems of equations. You also must be able to interpret, represent, and evaluate functions numerically, graphically, symbolically, and descriptively. In addition, you will have to identify the proper graphs of various functions, including translations, horizontal and vertical reflections, and symmetry about the x- and y- axes and about the origin. Finally, you must demonstrate a clear understanding of linear and exponential growth.

To demonstrate mastery of counting, you will be asked to properly utilize the multiplication rule, as well as use and identify combinations and permutations. For probability, you must understand the concepts of union, intersection, independent and mutually exclusive events, complementary events, conditional probabilities, and expected value.

In data analysis and statistics, you must be able to both interpret and represent data in various forms, including tables; bar, line and circle graphs; pie charts; scatterplots; and histograms. You must also be able to determine the mean, median, mode, and range of a set of data and answer conceptual questions related to standard deviation and normal distribution.

Financial mathematics focuses on percentages, interest, and value. For percentages, you should be able to calculate percent change, determine markups and discounts, apply taxes, and calculate profit and loss. You also must demonstrate mastery of the different types of interest—simple, compound, and continuous—and be able to determine the effective interest rate as well as the effective annual yield or annual percentage rate. In terms of value, you should be able to define and apply the concepts of present and future value.

Regarding geometry, the test will ask questions involving the properties of triangles and quadrilaterals, including perimeter, area, similarity, and the Pythagorean theorem. You also must understand the properties of parallel and perpendicular lines and the properties of circles, including circumference, area, central angles, inscribed angles, and sectors.

You will also be expected to show a solid understanding of logic and sets. You must be able to identify and apply a variety of logical operations and statement types, including conditional statements, conjunctions, disjunctions, negations, hypotheses, logical conclusions, converses, inverses, counterexamples, contrapositives, and logical equivalence. You must also understand sets: the relationships within and between them, subsets, disjoint sets, equality of sets, and Venn diagrams. In addition, you will need to complete operations on sets, including union, intersection, and complement.

Finally, you must demonstrate mastery of number systems—including both real and complex numbers—and understand the concept of absolute value. You must be able to recognize rational and irrational numbers and demonstrate basic number theory: factors and divisibility, primes and composites, odd and even integers, and the fundamental theorem of arithmetic. You also must be able to properly use unit conversion, scientific notation, and numerical precision in order to show that you have an accurate understanding of measurement.

How is the CLEP College Mathematics Exam Scored?

You will receive your scores on your CLEP College Mathematics Exam immediately upon your completion of the exam. At the end of the exam, you will have the option to not have your test scored. If you do not want your scores reported, select this option. It is important to note that you must make this choice BEFORE you have seen your score. Once you have seen your score, you cannot choose to have it cancelled.

Your CLEP scores will automatically be added to your CLEP transcript. When you register, you can pre-select the college or employer you would like to receive your scores. If you are taking the exam before you have decided where you are attending school, you can request your CLEP transcript when you are ready. The first transcript request is free regardless of when it is requested.

Each multiple-choice question is worth one raw point. The total number of questions you answer correctly is added up to obtain your raw score. The raw score is then scaled to a score between twenty and eighty. Minimum passing scores vary by institution, so it is important to check with your college or university.

There is no guessing penalty on the CLEP College Mathematics exam, so you should always guess if you do not know the answer to a question.

How is the CLEP College Mathematics Exam Administered?

The CLEP College Mathematics exam is a computer-based test offered at over 1,800 locations worldwide. There are four different types of test centers:

- Open test centers that will test any student who has registered and paid the fee.
- Limited test centers that are located at universities and colleges and will only test admitted or enrolled students.
- On-base test centers that are located in military installations and only test eligible service members and civilians with authorized access to the installation.
- Fully-funded test centers that are also only for military service members, eligible civilians, and their spouses. These centers administer exams for Defense Activity for Nontraditional Education Support (DANTES)-funded test-takers, who are exempt from the administrative fee.

Regardless of the type of test center, you must contact the test center directly to make a reservation to take the exam. Check https://clep.collegeboard.org/search/test-centers for more information.

You will need to print your registration ticket from your online account and bring it, along with your identification, to the testing site on the day of the exam. Some test centers will require other forms or documentation, so check with your test center in advance. Test centers may also require administrative fees in addition to the registration fee for the exam itself. No pens, pencils, erasers, printed, or written materials, electronic devices, or calculators are allowed. An online scientific calculator will be provided to you at the time of the test. You can access the calculator for free for thirty days before your test in order to familiarize yourself with it.

You may not bring a bag with you into the testing room. You are also forbidden to wear headwear (unless for religious purposes). You may take the test once every three months. Please note that DANTES does not fund retesting.

About This Guide

This guide will help you master the most important test topics and develop critical test-taking skills. We have built features into our books to prepare you for your tests and increase your score. Along with a detailed summary of the test's format, content, and scoring, we offer an in-depth overview of the content knowledge required to pass the test. In the content review sections, you'll find sidebars that provide interesting information, highlight key concepts, and review content so that you can solidify your understanding of the material that you will be tested on. You can also test your knowledge with sample questions throughout the text and practice questions that reflect the content and format of the CLEP College Mathematics exam. We're pleased you've chosen Accepted, Inc. to be a part of your college journey!

CHAPTER ONE
Numbers and Operations

This chapter provides a review of the basic yet critical components of mathematics such as manipulating fractions, comparing numbers, and using units. These concepts will provide the foundation for more complex mathematical operations in later chapters.

Types of Numbers

Numbers are placed in categories based on their properties.

- A **NATURAL NUMBER** is greater than 0 and has no decimal or fraction attached. These are also sometimes called counting numbers {1, 2, 3, 4, ...}.
- **WHOLE NUMBERS** are natural numbers and the number 0 {0, 1, 2, 3, 4, ...}.
- **INTEGERS** include positive and negative natural numbers and 0 {..., –4, –3, –2, –1, 0, 1, 2, 3, 4, ...}.
- A **RATIONAL NUMBER** can be represented as a fraction. Any decimal part must terminate or resolve into a repeating pattern. Examples include –12, $-\frac{4}{5}$, 0.36, $7.\overline{7}$, $26\frac{1}{2}$, etc.
- An **IRRATIONAL NUMBER** cannot be represented as a fraction. An irrational decimal number never ends and never resolves into a repeating pattern. Examples include $-\sqrt{7}$, π, and 0.34567989135...
- A **REAL NUMBER** is a number that can be represented by a point on a number line. Real numbers include all the rational and irrational numbers.
- An **IMAGINARY NUMBER** includes the imaginary unit i, where $i = \sqrt{-1}$ Because $i^2 = -1$, imaginary numbers produce a negative value when squared. Examples of imaginary numbers include $-4i$, $0.75i$, $i\sqrt{2}$ and $\frac{8}{3}i$.

- A **COMPLEX NUMBER** is in the form $a + bi$, where a and b are real numbers. Examples of complex numbers include $3 + 2i$, $-4 + i$, $\sqrt{3} - i\sqrt[3]{5}$ and $\frac{5}{8} - \frac{7i}{8}$. All imaginary numbers are also complex.

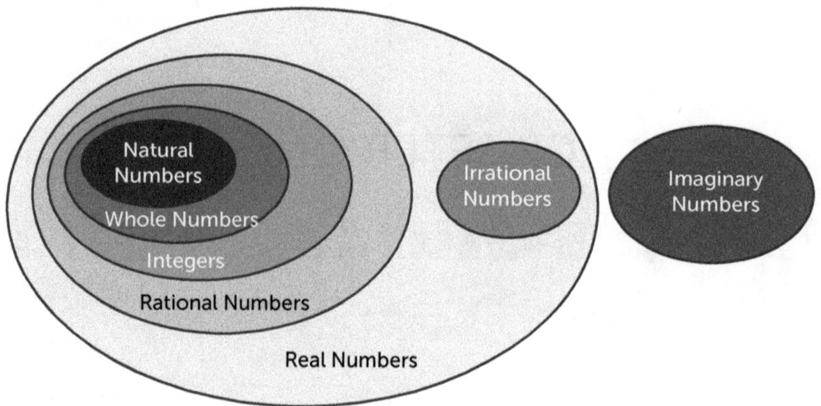

Figure 1.1. Types of Numbers

DID YOU KNOW?

If a real number is a natural number (e.g., 50), then it is also a whole number, an integer, and a rational number.

The **FACTORS** of a natural number are all the numbers that can multiply together to make the number. For example, the factors of 24 are 1, 2, 3, 4, 6, 8, 12, and 24. Every natural number is either prime or composite. A **PRIME NUMBER** is a number that is only divisible by itself and 1. (The number 1 is not considered prime.) Examples of prime numbers are 2, 3, 7, and 29. The number 2 is the only even prime number. A **COMPOSITE NUMBER** has more than two factors. For example, 6 is composite because its factors are 1, 6, 2, and 3. Every composite number can be written as a unique product of prime numbers, called the **PRIME FACTORIZATION** of the number. For example, the prime factorization of 90 is $90 = 2 \times 3^2 \times 5$. All integers are either even or odd. An even number is divisible by 2; an odd number is not.

PROPERTIES of NUMBER SYSTEMS

A system is **CLOSED** under an operation if performing that operation on two elements of the system results in another element of that system. For example, the integers are closed under the operations of addition, subtraction, and multiplication but not division. Adding, subtracting, or multiplying two integers results in another integer. However, dividing two integers could result in a rational number that is not an integer $\left(-2 \div 3 = \frac{-2}{3}\right)$.

- The rational numbers are closed under all four operations (except for division by 0).
- The real numbers are closed under all four operations.
- The complex numbers are closed under all four operations.

- The irrational numbers are NOT closed under ANY of the four operations.

The **COMMUTATIVE PROPERTY** holds for an operation if order does not matter when performing the operation. For example, multiplication is commutative for integers: $(-2)(3) = (3)(-2)$.

The **ASSOCIATIVE PROPERTY** holds for an operation if elements can be regrouped without changing the result. For example, addition is associative for real numbers: $-3 + (-5 + 4) = (-3 + -5) + 4$.

The **DISTRIBUTIVE PROPERTY** of multiplication over addition allows a product of sums to be written as a sum of products: $a(b + c) = ab + ac$. The value a is distributed over the sum $(b + c)$. The acronym FOIL (First, Outer, Inner, Last) is a useful way to remember the distributive property.

When an operation is performed with an **IDENTITY ELEMENT** and another element a, the result is a. The identity element for multiplication on real numbers is $a \times 1 = a$), and for addition is 0 ($a + 0 = a$).

An operation of a system has an **INVERSE ELEMENT** if applying that operation with the inverse element results in the identity element. For example, the inverse element of a for addition is $-a$ because $a + (-a) = 0$. The inverse element of a for multiplication is $\frac{1}{a}$ because $a \times \frac{1}{a} = 1$.

EXAMPLES

1. Classify the following numbers as natural, whole, integer, rational, or irrational. (The numbers may have more than one classification.)

[A] 72

[B] $-\frac{2}{3}$

[C] $\sqrt{5}$

2. Determine the real and imaginary parts of the following complex numbers.

[A] 20

[B] $10 - i$

[C] $15i$

3. Answer True or False for each statement:

[A] The natural numbers are closed under subtraction.

[B] The sum of two irrational numbers is irrational.

[C] The sum of a rational number and an irrational number is irrational.

4. Answer true or false for each statement:

[A] The associative property applies for multiplication in the real numbers.

[B] The commutative property applies to all real numbers and all operations.

OPERATIONS with COMPLEX NUMBERS

Operations with complex numbers are similar to operations with real numbers in that complex numbers can be added, subtracted, multiplied, and divided. When adding or subtracting, the imaginary parts and real parts are combined separately. When multiplying, the distributive property (FOIL) can be applied. Note that multiplying complex numbers often creates the value i^2 which can be simplified to –1.

To divide complex numbers, multiply both the top and bottom of the fraction by the **COMPLEX CONJUGATE** of the divisor (bottom number). The complex conjugate is the complex number with the sign of the imaginary part changed. For example, the complex conjugate of $3 + 4i$ would be $3 - 4i$. Since both the top and the bottom of the fraction are multiplied by the same number, the fraction is really just being multiplied by 1. When simplified, the denominator of the fraction will now be a real number.

EXAMPLES

5. Simplify: $(3 - 2i) - (-2 + 8i)$

6. Simplify: $\frac{4i}{(5-2i)}$

Scientific Notation

SCIENTIFIC NOTATION is a method of representing very large and small numbers in the form $a \times 10^n$, where a is a value between 1 and 10, and n is a nonzero integer. For example, the number 927,000,000 is written in scientific notation as 9.27×10^8. Multiplying 9.27 by 10 eight times gives 927,000,000. When performing operations with scientific notation, the final answer should be in the form $a \times 10^n$.

65000000.
7 6 5 4 3 2 1
↓
6.5×10^7

.0000987
–1–2–3–4–5
↓
9.87×10^{-5}

Figure 1.2. Scientific Notation

DID YOU KNOW?
When multiplying numbers in scientific notation, add the exponents. When dividing, subtract the exponents.

When adding and subtracting numbers in scientific notation, the power of 10 must be the same for all numbers. This results in like terms in which the a terms are added or subtracted and the 10^n remains unchanged. When multiplying numbers in scientific notation, multiply the a factors, and then multiply that answer by 10 to the sum of the exponents. For division, divide the a factors and subtract the exponents.

EXAMPLES

7. Simplify: $(3.8 \times 10^3) + (4.7 \times 10^2)$

8. Simplify: $(8.1 \times 10^{-5})(1.4 \times 10^7)$

Order of Operations

The **ORDER OF OPERATIONS** is simply the order in which operations are performed. Multiplication and division, and addition and subtraction, are performed together from left to right. So, performing multiple operations on a set of numbers is a four-step process. **PEMDAS** is a common way to remember the order of operations:

1. **P**arentheses: Calculate expressions inside parentheses, brackets, braces, etc.
2. **E**xponents: Calculate exponents and square roots.
3. **M**ultiplication: Calculate any remaining multiplication and division in order from left to right.
4. **D**ivision: Calculate any remaining multiplication and division in order from left to right.
5. **A**ddition: Calculate any remaining addition and subtraction in order from left to right.
6. **S**ubtraction: Calculate any remaining addition and subtraction in order from left to right.

Always work from left to right within each step when simplifying expressions.

EXAMPLES

9. Simplify: $2(21 - 14) + 6 \div (-2) \times 3 - 10$

10. Simplify: $-(3)^2 + 4(5) + (5 - 6)^2 - 8$

11. Simplify: $\frac{(7 - 9)^3 + 8(10 - 12)}{4^2 - 5^2}$

Units of Measurement

The standard units for the metric and American systems are shown below, along with the prefixes used to express metric units.

Table 1.1. Units and Conversion Factors

Dimension	American	SI
length	inch/foot/yard/mile	meter
mass	ounce/pound/ton	gram
volume	cup/pint/quart/gallon	liter
force	pound-force	newton
pressure	pound-force per square inch	pascal
work and energy	cal/British thermal unit	joule

Table 1.1. Units and Conversion Factors (continued)		
DIMENSION	AMERICAN	SI
temperature	Fahrenheit	kelvin
charge	faraday	coulomb

Table 1.2. Metric Prefixes		
PREFIX	SYMBOL	MULTIPLICATION FACTOR
tera	T	1,000,000,000,000
giga	G	1,000,000,000
mega	M	1,000,000
kilo	k	1,000
hecto	h	100
deca	da	10
base unit	--	--
deci	d	0.1
centi	c	0.01
milli	m	0.001
micro	μ	0.000001
nano	n	0.000000001
pico	p	0.000000000001

Units can be converted within a single system or between systems. When converting from one unit to another unit, a conversion factor (a numeric multiplier used to convert a value with a unit to another unit) is used. The process of converting between units using a conversion factor is sometimes known as dimensional analysis.

Table 1.3. Conversion Factors	
1 in. = 2.54 cm	1 lb. = 0.454 kg
1 yd. = 0.914 m	1 cal = 4.19 J
1 mi. = 1.61 km	$1^{\circ}F = \frac{9}{5}{}^{\circ}C + 32^{\circ}C$
1 gal. = 3.785 L	$1\ cm^3 = 1\ mL$
1 oz. = 28.35 g	1 hr = 3600 s

EXAMPLES

12. Convert the following measurements in the metric system.

[A] 4.25 kilometers to meters

[B] 8 m^2 to mm^2

13. Convert the following measurements in the American system.

[A] 12 feet to inches

[B] 7 yd^2 to ft^2

14. Convert the following measurements in the metric system to the American system.

[A] 23 meters to feet

[B] 10 m^2 to yd^2

15. Convert the following measurements in the American system to the metric system.

[A] 8 in^3 to milliliters

[B] 16 kilograms to pounds

Fractions

A **FRACTION** is a number that can be written in the form $\frac{a}{b}$, where b is not equal to 0. The a part of the fraction is the **NUMERATOR** (top number) and the b part of the fraction is the **DENOMINATOR** (bottom number).

If the denominator of a fraction is greater than the numerator, the value of the fraction is less than 1 and it is called a **PROPER FRACTION** (for example, $\frac{3}{5}$ is a proper fraction). In an **IMPROPER FRACTION**, the denominator is less than the numerator and the value of the fraction is greater than 1 ($\frac{8}{3}$ is an improper fraction). An improper fraction can be written as a **MIXED NUMBER**, which has a whole number part and a proper fraction part. Improper fractions can be converted to mixed numbers by dividing the numerator by the denominator, which gives the whole number part, and the remainder becomes the numerator of the proper fraction part. (For example, the improper fraction $\frac{25}{9}$ is equal to mixed number $2\frac{7}{9}$ because 9 divides into 25 two times, with a remainder of 7.)

Conversely, mixed numbers can be converted to improper fractions. To do so, determine the numerator of the improper fraction by multiplying the denominator by the whole number, and then adding the numerator. The final number is written as the (now larger) numerator over the original denominator.

DID YOU KNOW?

To convert mixed numbers to improper fractions:

$a\frac{m}{n} = \frac{n \times a + m}{n}$

Fractions with the same denominator can be added or subtracted by simply adding or subtracting the numerators; the denominator will remain unchanged. To add or subtract fractions with different denominators, find the **LEAST**

COMMON DENOMINATOR (LCD) of all the fractions. The LCD is the smallest number exactly divisible by each denominator. (For example, the least common denominator of the numbers 2, 3, and 8 is 24.) Once the LCD has been found, each fraction should be written in an equivalent form with the LCD as the denominator.

To multiply fractions, the numerators are multiplied together and denominators are multiplied together. If there are any mixed numbers, they should first be changed to improper fractions. Then, the numerators are multiplied together and the denominators are multiplied together. The fraction can then be reduced if necessary. To divide fractions, multiply the first fraction by the reciprocal of the second.

DID YOU KNOW?

$\frac{a}{b} \pm \frac{c}{b} = \frac{a \pm c}{b}$

$\frac{a}{b} \times \frac{c}{d} = \frac{ac}{bd}$

$\frac{a}{b} \div \frac{c}{d} = \left(\frac{a}{b}\right)\left(\frac{d}{c}\right) = \frac{ad}{bc}$

Any common denominator can be used to add or subtract fractions. The quickest way to find a common denominator of a set of values is simply to multiply all the values together. The result might not be the least common denominator, but it will allow the problem to be worked.

EXAMPLES

16. Simplify: $2\frac{3}{5} + 3\frac{1}{4} - 1\frac{1}{2}$

17. Simplify: $\frac{7}{8} \times 3\frac{1}{3}$

18. Simplify: $4\frac{1}{2} \div \frac{2}{3}$

Ratios

A **RATIO** is a comparison of two numbers and can be represented as $\frac{a}{b}$, a:b, or a to b. The two numbers represent a constant relationship, not a specific value: for every a number of items in the first group, there will be b number of items in the second. For example, if the ratio of blue to red candies in a bag is 3:5, the bag will contain 3 blue candies for every 5 red candies. So, the bag might contain 3 blue candies and 5 red candies, or it might contain 30 blue candies and 50 red candies, or 36 blue candies and 60 red candies. All of these values are representative of the ratio 3:5 (which is the ratio in its lowest, or simplest, terms).

To find the "whole" when working with ratios, simply add the values in the ratio. For example, if the ratio of boys to girls in a class is 2:3, the "whole" is five: 2 out of every 5 students are boys, and 3 out of every 5 students are girls.

EXAMPLES

19. There are 10 boys and 12 girls in a first-grade class. What is the ratio of boys to the total number of students? What is the ratio of girls to boys?

20. A family spends $600 a month on rent, $400 on utilities, $750 on groceries, and $550 on miscellaneous expenses. What is the ratio of the family's rent to their total expenses?

Proportions

A **PROPORTION** is an equation which states that two ratios are equal. A proportion is given in the form $\frac{a}{b} = \frac{c}{d}$, where the a and d terms are the extremes and the b and c terms are the means. A proportion is solved using cross-multiplication ($ad = bc$) to create an equation with no fractional components. A proportion must have the same units in both numerators and both denominators.

EXAMPLES

21. Solve the proportion for x: $\frac{3x-5}{2} = \frac{x-8}{3}$.

22. A map is drawn such that 2.5 inches on the map equates to an actual distance of 40 miles. If the distance measured on the map between two cities is 17.25 inches, what is the actual distance between them in miles?

23. A factory knows that 4 out of 1000 parts made will be defective. If in a month there are 125,000 parts made, how many of these parts will be defective?

Percentages

A **PERCENT** (or percentage) means per hundred and is expressed with a percent symbol (%). For example, 54% means 54 out of every 100. A percent can be converted to a decimal by removing the % symbol and moving the decimal point two places to the left, while a decimal can be converted to a percent by moving the decimal point two places to the right and attaching the % sign. A percent can be converted to a fraction by writing the percent as a fraction with 100 as the denominator and reducing. A fraction can be converted to a percent by performing the indicated division, multiplying the result by 100, and attaching the % sign.

The equation for finding percentages has three variables: the part, the whole, and the percent (which is expressed in the equation as a decimal). The equation, as shown below, can be rearranged to solve for any of these variables.

- part = whole × percent
- percent = $\frac{\text{part}}{\text{whole}}$
- whole = $\frac{\text{part}}{\text{percent}}$

This set of equations can be used to solve percent word problems. All that's needed is to identify the part, whole, and/or percent, and then to plug those values into the appropriate equation and solve.

EXAMPLES

24. Change the following values to the indicated form:

[A] 18% to a fraction

[B] $\frac{3}{5}$ to a percent

[C] 1.125 to a percent

[D] 84% to a decimal

25. In a school of 650 students, 54% of the students are boys. How many students are girls?

PERCENT CHANGE

Percent change problems involve a change from an original amount. Often percent change problems appear as word problems that include discounts, growth, or markups.

DID YOU KNOW?

Key terms associated with percent change problems include *discount*, *sales tax*, and *markup*.

In order to solve percent change problems, it's necessary to identify the percent change (as a decimal), the amount of change, and the original amount. (Keep in mind that one of these will be the value being solved for.) These values can then be plugged into the equations below:

- amount of change = original amount × percent change
- $\text{percent change} = \frac{\text{amount of change}}{\text{original amount}}$
- $\text{original amount} = \frac{\text{amount of change}}{\text{percent change}}$

EXAMPLES

26. An HDTV that originally cost $1,500 is on sale for 45% off. What is the sale price for the item?

27. A house was bought in 2000 for $100,000 and sold in 2015 for $120,000. What was the percent growth in the value of the house from 2000 to 2015?

Exponents and Radicals

EXPONENTS

An expression in the form b^n is in an exponential notation where b is the **BASE** and n is an **EXPONENT.** To perform the operation, multiply the base by itself the number of times indicated by the exponent. For example, 2^3 is equal to $2 \times 2 \times 2$ or 8.

Table 1.4. Operations with Exponents

Rule	Example	Explanation
$a^0 = 1$	$5^0 = 1$	Any base (except 0) to the 0 power is 1.
$a^{-n} = \frac{1}{a^n}$	$5^{-3} = \frac{1}{5^3}$	A negative exponent becomes positive when moved from numerator to denominator (or vice versa).
$a^m a^n = a^{m+n}$	$5^3 5^4 = 5^{3+4} = 5^7$	Add the exponents to multiply two powers with the same base.
$(a^m)^n = a^{m \times n}$	$(5^3)^4 = 5^{3(4)} = 5^{12}$	Multiply the exponents to raise a power to a power.
$\frac{a^m}{a^n} = a^{m-n}$	$\frac{5^4}{5^3} = 5^{4-3} = 5^1$	Subtract the exponents to divide two powers with the same base.
$(ab)^n = a^n b^n$	$(5 \times 6)^3 = 5^3 6^3$	Apply the exponent to each base to raise a product to a power.
$\left(\frac{a}{b}\right)^n = \frac{a^n}{b^n}$	$\left(\frac{5}{6}\right)^3 = \frac{5^3}{6^3}$	Apply the exponent to each base to raise a quotient to a power.
$\left(\frac{a}{b}\right)^{-n} = \left(\frac{b}{a}\right)^n$	$\left(\frac{5}{6}\right)^{-3} = \left(\frac{6}{5}\right)^3$	Invert the fraction and change the sign of the exponent to raise a fraction to a negative power.
$\frac{a^m}{b^n} = \frac{b^{-n}}{a^{-m}}$	$\frac{5^3}{6^4} = \frac{6^{-4}}{5^{-3}}$	Change the sign of the exponent when moving a number from the numerator to denominator (or vice versa).

EXAMPLES

28. Simplify: $\frac{(10^2)^3}{(10^2)^2}$

29. Simplify: $\frac{(x^{-2}y^2)^2}{x^3y}$

RADICALS

RADICALS are expressed as $\sqrt[b]{a}$, where b is called the **INDEX** and a is the **RADICAND.** A radical is used to indicate the inverse operation of an exponent: finding the base which can be raised to b to yield a. For example, $\sqrt[3]{125}$ is equal to 5 because 5 × 5 × 5 equals 125. The same operation can be expressed using a fraction exponent, so $\sqrt[b]{a} = a^{\frac{1}{b}}$. Note that when no value is indicated for b, it is assumed to be 2 (square root).

When b is even and a is positive, $\sqrt[b]{a}$ is defined to be the positive real value n such that $nb = a$ (example: $\sqrt{16} = 4$ only, and not −4, even though $(-4)(-4) = 16$). If b is even and a is negative, $\sqrt[b]{a}$ will be a complex number (example: $\sqrt{-9} = 3i$). Finally if b is odd, $\sqrt[b]{a}$ will always be a real number regardless of the sign of a. If a is negative, $\sqrt[b]{a}$ will be negative since a number to an odd power is negative (example: $\sqrt[5]{-32} = -2$ since $(-2)^5 = -32$).

$\sqrt[n]{x}$ is referred to as the nth root of x.

- $n = 2$ is the square root
- $n = 3$ is the cube root
- $n = 4$ is the fourth root
- $n = 5$ is the fifth root

The following table of operations with radicals holds for all cases EXCEPT the case where b is even and a is negative (the complex case).

Table 1.5. Operations with Radicals

Rule	Example	Explanation
$\sqrt[b]{ac} = \sqrt[b]{a}\sqrt[b]{c}$	$\sqrt[3]{81} = \sqrt[3]{27}\sqrt[3]{3} = 3\sqrt[3]{3}$	The values under the radical sign can be separated into values that multiply to the original value.
$\sqrt[b]{\frac{a}{c}} = \frac{\sqrt[b]{a}}{\sqrt[b]{c}}$	$\sqrt{\frac{4}{81}} = \frac{\sqrt{4}}{\sqrt{81}} = \frac{2}{9}$	The b-root of the numerator and denominator can be calculated when there is a fraction under a radical sign.
$\sqrt[b]{a^c} = (\sqrt[b]{a})^c = a^{\frac{c}{b}}$	$\sqrt[3]{6^2} = (\sqrt[3]{6})^2 = 6^{\frac{2}{3}}$	The b-root can be written as a fractional exponent. If there is a power under the radical sign, it will be the numerator of the fraction.
$\frac{c}{\sqrt[b]{a}} \times \frac{\sqrt[b]{a}}{\sqrt[b]{a}} = \frac{c\sqrt[b]{a}}{a}$	$\frac{5}{\sqrt{2}}\frac{\sqrt{2}}{\sqrt{2}} = \frac{5\sqrt{2}}{2}$	To rationalize the denominator, multiply the numerator and denominator by the radical in the denominator until the radical has been canceled out.
$\frac{c}{b-\sqrt{a}} \times \frac{b+\sqrt{a}}{b+\sqrt{a}} = \frac{c(b+\sqrt{a})}{b^2-a}$	$\frac{4}{3-\sqrt{2}}\frac{3+\sqrt{2}}{3+\sqrt{2}} = \frac{4(3+\sqrt{2})}{9-2} = \frac{12+4\sqrt{2}}{7}$	To rationalize the denominator, the numerator and denominator are multiplied by the conjugate of the denominator.

EXAMPLES

30. Simplify: $\sqrt{48}$

31. Simplify: $\frac{6}{\sqrt{8}}$

Factorials

A **FACTORIAL** of a number n is denoted by $n!$ and is equal to $1 \times 2 \times 3 \times 4 \times \ldots \times n$. Both 0! and 1! are equal to 1 by definition. Fractions containing factorials can often be simplified by crossing out the portions of the factorials that occur in both the numerator and denominator.

EXAMPLES

32. Simplify: 8!

33. Simplify: $\frac{10!}{7!3!}$

Sequences and Series

Sequences can be thought of as a set of numbers (called **TERMS**) with a rule that explains the particular pattern between the terms. The terms of a sequence are separated by commas. There are two types of sequences that will be examined, arithmetic and geometric. The sum of an arithmetic sequence is known as an **ARITHMETIC SERIES**; similarly the sum of a geometric sequence is known as a **GEOMETRIC SERIES**.

ARITHMETIC SEQUENCES

ARITHMETIC GROWTH is constant growth, meaning that the difference between any one term in the series and the next consecutive term will be the same constant. This constant is called the **COMMON DIFFERENCE**. Thus, to list the terms in the sequence, one can just add (or subtract) the same number repeatedly. For example, the series {20, 30, 40, 50} is arithmetic since 10 is added each time to get from one term to the next. One way to represent this sequence is using a **RECURSIVE** definition, which basically says: *next term = current term + common difference*. For this example, the recursive definition would be $a_{n+1} = a_n + 10$ because the *next* term a_{n+1} in the sequence is the current term a_n plus 10. In general, the recursive definition of a series is:

$a_{n+1} = a_n + d$, where d is the common difference.

Often, the objective of arithmetic sequence questions is to find a specific term in the sequence or the sum of a certain series of terms. The formulas to use are:

Table 1.6. Formulas for Arithmetic Sequences and Series

Finding the *n*th term . . .	
$a_n = a_1 + d(n - 1)$ $a_n = a_m + d(n - m)$	d = the common difference of the sequence a_n = the nth term in the sequence n = the number of the term a_m = the mth term in the sequence m = the number of the term a_1 = the first term in the sequence
Finding the partial sum . . .	
$S_n = \frac{n(a_1 + a_n)}{2}$	S_n = sum of the terms through the nth term a_n = the nth term in the sequence n = the number of the term a_1 = the first term in the sequence

EXAMPLES

34. Find the ninth term of the sequence: −57, −40, −23, −6 ...

35. If the 23rd term in an arithmetic sequence is 820, and the 5th term is 200, find the common difference between each term.

36. Evaluate $\sum_{n=14}^{45} 2n + 10$.

GEOMETRIC SEQUENCES

While an arithmetic sequence has an additive pattern, a **GEOMETRIC SEQUENCE** has a multiplicative pattern. This means that to get from any one term in the sequence to the next term in the sequence, the term is multiplied by a fixed number (called the **COMMON RATIO**). The following sequence is a geometric sequence: {8, 4, 2, 1, .5, .25, .125}. In this case, the multiplier (or common ratio) is $\frac{1}{2}$. The multiplier can be any real number other than 0 or 1. To find the common ratio, simply choose any term in the sequence and divide it by the previous term (this is the ratio of two consecutive terms—thus the name common *ratio*). In the above example, the ratio between the second and third terms is $\frac{2}{4} = \frac{1}{2}$.

Geometric sequences require their own formulas to find the next term and a sum of a specific series.

Table 1.7. Geometric Sequences: Formulas

Finding the *n*th term . . .	
$a_n = a_1 \times r^{n-1}$ $a_n = a_m \times r^{n-m}$	r = the common ratio of the sequence a_n = the nth term in the sequence n = the number of the term a_m = the mth term in the sequence m = the number of the term a_1 = the first term in the sequence
Finding the partial sum . . .	
$S_n = \frac{a_1(1-r^n)}{1-r}$	S_n = sum of the terms through the nth term r = the common ratio of the sequence a_n = the nth term in the sequence n = the number of the term a_1 = the first term in the sequence
Finding the sum of an infinite series . . .	
$S_\infty = \frac{a}{1-r}$ $(\lvert r \rvert < 1)$	S_∞ = sum of all terms r = the common ratio of the sequence a = the fifth term in the sequence

The finite sum formula works similarly to the arithmetic sequence sum. However, sometimes the **INFINITE SUM** of the sequence must be found. The sum of an infinite number of terms of a sequence is called a **SERIES.** If the infinite terms of the sequence add up to a finite number, the series is said to **CONVERGE** to that number. If the sum of the terms is infinite, then the series **DIVERGES.** Another way to say this is to ask: is there a limit to the finite sum S_n as n goes to infinity? For geometric series in the form $\sum_{n=1}^{\infty} a \times r^n$, the series converges only when $|r| < 1$ (or $-1 < r < 1$). If r is greater than 1, the sum will approach infinity, so the series diverges.

DID YOU KNOW?

Compared to arithmetic growth, geometric growth is much faster. As seen in the formulas used to find a geometric term, geometric growth is exponential, whereas arithmetic growth is linear.

EXAMPLES

37. Find the 8th term in the sequence: {13, 39, 117, 351 . . .}

38. Find the sum of the first 10 terms of this sequence: {–4, 16, –64, 256 . . .}

Test Your Knowledge

Work the problem, and then choose the most correct answer.

1. Simplify: $\frac{7.2 \times 10^6}{1.6 \times 10^{-3}}$
   - **A)** 4.5×10^{-9}
   - **B)** 4.5×10^{-3}
   - **C)** 4.5×10^{3}
   - **D)** 4.5×10^{9}

2. Simplify: $(3^2 \div 1^3) - (4 - 8^2) + 2^4$
   - **A)** −35
   - **B)** −4
   - **C)** 28
   - **D)** 85

3. In a theater, there are 4,500 lower-level seats and 2,000 upper-level seats. What is the ratio of lower-level seats to total seats?
   - **A)** $\frac{4}{9}$
   - **B)** $\frac{4}{13}$
   - **C)** $\frac{9}{13}$
   - **D)** $\frac{9}{4}$

4. If a student answers 42 out of 48 questions correctly on a quiz, what percentage of questions did she answer correctly?
   - **A)** 82.5%
   - **B)** 85%
   - **C)** 87.5%
   - **D)** 90%

5. A worker was paid $15,036 for 7 months of work. If he received the same amount each month, how much was he paid for the first 2 months?
   - **A)** $2,148
   - **B)** $4,296
   - **C)** $6,444
   - **D)** $8,592

6. Simplify: $\frac{(3x^2y^2)^2}{3^3x^{-2}y^3}$
   - **A)** $3x^6y$
   - **B)** $\frac{x^6y}{3}$
   - **C)** $\frac{x^4}{3y}$
   - **D)** $\frac{3x^4}{y}$

7. Simplify: $\frac{5^2(3) + 3(-2)^2}{4 + 3^2 - 2(5 - 8)}$

   Write in the answer:

   ____

8. Convert 55 meters to feet (round to the nearest tenth of a foot).

   Write in the answer:

   ____

Answer Key

EXAMPLES

1. [A] **The number is natural, whole, an integer, and rational.**

[B] **The fraction is rational.**

[C] **The number is irrational.** (It cannot be written as a fraction, and written as a decimal is approximately 2.2360679...)

2. A complex number is in the form of $a + bi$, where a is the real part and bi is the imaginary part.

[A] $20 = 20 + 0i$

The real part is 20, and there is no imaginary part.

[B] $10 - i = 10 - 1i$

The real part is 10, and $-1i$ is the imaginary part.

[C] $15i = 0 + 15i$

The real part is 0, and the imaginary part is $15i$.

3. **[A] is false.** Subtracting the natural number 7 from 2 results in $2 - 7 = -5$, which is an integer, but not a natural number.

[B] is false. For example, $(5 - 2\sqrt{3}) + (2 + 2\sqrt{3}) = 7$. The sum of two irrational numbers in this example is a whole number, which is not irrational. The sum of a rational number and an irrational number is sometimes rational and sometimes irrational.

[C] is true. Because irrational numbers have decimal parts that are unending and with no pattern, adding a repeating or terminating decimal will still result in an unending decimal without a pattern.

4. **[A] is true.** For all real numbers, $a \times (b \times c) = (a \times b) \times c$. Order of multiplication does not change the result.

[B] is false. The commutative property does not work for subtraction or division on real numbers. For example, $12 - 5 = 7$, but $5 - 12 = -7$, and $10 \div 2 = 5$, but $2 \div 10 = \frac{1}{5}$.

5. $(3 - 2i) - (-2 + 8i)$

Distribute the −1.

$= (3 - 2i) - 1(-2 + 8i)$

$= 3 - 2i + 2 - 8i$

Combine like terms.

$\mathbf{= 5 - 10i}$

6. $\frac{4i}{(5 - 2i)}$

Multiply the top and bottom of the fraction by the complex conjugate of $5 + 2i$.

$= \frac{4i}{5 - 2i}\left(\frac{5 + 2i}{5 + 2i}\right)$

$= \frac{20i + 8i^2}{25 + 10i - 10i - 4i^2}$

Simplify the result using the identity $i^2 = -1$.

$= \frac{20i + 8(-1)}{25 + 10i - 10i - 4(-1)}$

$= \frac{20i - 8}{25 + 10i - 10i + 4}$

Combine like terms.

$= \frac{20i - 8}{29}$

Write the answer in the form $a + bi$.

$= \mathbf{-\frac{8}{29} + \frac{20}{29}i}$

7. $(3.8 \times 10^3) + (4.7 \times 10^2)$

To add, the exponents of 10 must be the same.

$3.8 \times 10^3 = 3.8 \times 10 \times 10^2 = 38 \times 10^2$

Add the *a* terms together.

$38 \times 10^2 + 4.7 \times 10^2 = 42.7 \times 10^2$

Write the number in proper scientific notation.

$= 4.27 \times 10^3$

8. $(8.1 \times 10^{-5})(1.4 \times 10^7)$

Multiply the *a* factors and add the exponents on the base of 10.

$8.1 \times 1.4 = 11.34$

$-5 + 7 = 2$

$= 11.34 \times 10^2$

Write the number in proper scientific notation.

$= 1.134 \times 10^3$

9. $2(21 - 14) + 6 \div (-2) \times 3 - 10$

Calculate expressions inside parentheses.

$= 2(7) + 6 \div (-2) \times 3 - 10$

There are no exponents or radicals, so perform multiplication and division from left to right.

$= 14 + 6 \div (-2) \times 3 - 10$

$= 14 + (-3) \times 3 - 10$

$= 14 + (-9) - 10$

Perform addition and subtraction from left to right.

$= 5 - 10 =$ **-5**

10. $-(3)^2 + 4(5) + (5 - 6)^2 - 8$

Calculate expressions inside parentheses.

$= -(3)^2 + 4(5) + (-1)^2 - 8$

Simplify exponents and radicals.

$= -9 + 4(5) + 1 - 8$

Perform multiplication and division from left to right.

$= -9 + 20 + 1 - 8$

Perform addition and subtraction from left to right.

$= 11 + 1 - 8$

$= 12 - 8 =$ **4**

11. Simplify: $\frac{(7-9)^3 + 8(10-12)}{4^2 - 5^2}$

Calculate expressions inside parentheses.

$= \frac{(-2)^3 + 8(-2)}{4^2 - 5^2}$

Simplify exponents and radicals.

$= \frac{-8 + (-16)}{16 - 25}$

Perform addition and subtraction from left to right.

$= \frac{-24}{-9}$

Simplify.

$= \mathbf{\frac{8}{3}}$

12. [A] $4.25 \text{ km} \left(\frac{1000 \text{ m}}{1 \text{ km}}\right) =$ **4250 m**

[B] $\frac{8 \text{ m}^2}{1} \times \frac{1000 \text{ mm}}{1 \text{ m}} \times \frac{1000 \text{ mm}}{1 \text{ m}} =$

8,000,000 mm²

Since the units are square units (m²), multiply by the conversion factor twice, so that both meters cancel.

13. [A] $12 \text{ ft}\left(\frac{12 \text{ in}}{1 \text{ ft}}\right) =$ **144 in**

[B] $7 \text{ yd}^2\left(\frac{3 \text{ ft}^2}{1 \text{ yd}^2}\right)\left(\frac{3 \text{ ft}^2}{1 \text{ yd}^2}\right) =$ **63 ft²**

Since the units are square units (ft²), multiply by the conversion factor twice.

14. [A] $23 \text{ m} \left(\frac{3.28 \text{ ft}}{1 \text{ m}}\right) =$ **75.44 ft**

[B] $\frac{10 \text{ m}^2}{1} \times \frac{1.094 \text{ yd}}{1 \text{ m}} \times \frac{1.094 \text{ yd}}{1 \text{ m}} =$

11.97 yd²

15. [A] $8 \text{ in}^3 \left(\frac{16.39 \text{ ml}}{1 \text{ in}^3}\right) =$ **131.12 mL**

[B] $16 \text{ kg}\left(\frac{2.2 \text{ lb}}{1 \text{ kg}}\right) =$ **35.2 lb**

16. $2\frac{3}{5} + 3\frac{1}{4} - 1\frac{1}{2}$

Change each fraction so it has a denominator of 20, which is the LCD of 5, 4, and 2.

$2 + 3 - 1 = 4$

$\frac{12}{20} + \frac{5}{20} - \frac{10}{20} = \frac{7}{20}$

Combine to get the final answer (a mixed number).

$\mathbf{4\frac{7}{20}}$

17. $\frac{7}{8} \times 3\frac{1}{3}$

Change the mixed number to an improper fraction.

$3\frac{1}{3} = \frac{10}{3}$

Multiply the numerators together and the denominators together.

$\frac{7}{8}\left(\frac{10}{3}\right) = \frac{7 \times 10}{8 \times 3} = \frac{70}{24}$

Reduce the fraction.

$= \frac{35}{12} = \mathbf{2\frac{11}{12}}$

18. $4\frac{1}{2} \div \frac{2}{3}$

Change the mixed number to an improper fraction.

$4\frac{1}{2} = \frac{9}{2}$

Multiply the first fraction by the reciprocal of the second fraction.

$\frac{9}{2} \div \frac{2}{3} = \frac{9}{2} \times \frac{3}{2} = \frac{27}{4}$

Simplify.

$= \mathbf{6\frac{3}{4}}$

19. Identify the variables.

number of boys: 10

number of girls: 12

number of students: 22

Write out and simplify the ratio of boys to total students.

number of boys : number of students

$= 10 : 22 = \frac{10}{22} = \mathbf{\frac{5}{11}}$

Write out and simplify the ratio of girls to boys.

number of girls : number of boys

$= 12 : 10 = \frac{12}{10} = \mathbf{\frac{6}{5}}$

20. Identify the variables.

rent = 600

utilities = 400

groceries = 750

miscellaneous = 550

total expenses =

600 + 400 + 750 + 550 = 2300

Write out and simplify the ratio of rent to total expenses.

rent : total expenses

$= 600 : 2300 = \frac{60}{2300} = \mathbf{\frac{6}{23}}$

21. $\frac{(3x - 5)}{2} = \frac{(x - 8)}{3}$

Cross-multiply.

$3(3x - 5) = 2(x - 8)$

Solve the equation for x.

$9x - 15 = 2x - 16$

$7x - 15 = -16$

$7x = -1$

$\mathbf{x = -\frac{1}{7}}$

22. Write a proportion where x equals the actual distance and each ratio is written as inches : miles.

$\frac{2.5}{40} = \frac{17.25}{x}$

Cross-multiply and divide to solve for x.

$2.5x = 690$

$x = 276$

The two cities are **276 miles apart**.

23. Write a proportion where x is the number of defective parts made and both ratios are written as defective : total.

$\frac{4}{1000} = \frac{x}{125{,}000}$

Cross-multiply and divide to solve for x.

$1000x = 500{,}000$

$x = 500$

There are **500 defective parts** for the month.

24. [A] The percent is written as a fraction over 100 and reduced:

$\frac{18}{100} = \mathbf{\frac{9}{50}}$

[B] Dividing 5 by 3 gives the value 0.6, which is then multiplied by 100: **60%**.

[C] The decimal point is moved two places to the right: $1.125 \times 100 =$ **112.5%**.

[D]The decimal point is moved two places to the left: $84 \div 100 =$ **0.84**.

25. Identify the variables.

Percent of students who are girls = 100% – 54% = 46%

percent = 46% = 0.46

whole = 650 students

part = ?

Plug the variables into the appropriate equation.

part = whole × percent

$= 0.46 \times 650 = 299$

There are 299 girls.

26. Identify the variables.

original amount =$1,500

percent change = 45% = 0.45

amount of change = ?

Plug the variables into the appropriate equation.

amount of change = original amount × percent change

$= 1500 \times 0.45 = 675$

To find the new price, subtract the amount of change from the original price.

$1500 - 675 = 825$

The final price is $825.

27. Identify the variables.

original amount = $100,000

amount of change = 120,000 – 100,000 = 20,000

percent change = ?

Plug the variables into the appropriate equation.

$\text{percent change} = \frac{\text{amount of change}}{\text{original amount}}$

$= \frac{20{,}000}{100{,}000} = 0.20$

To find the percent growth, multiply by 100.

$0.20 \times 100 =$ **20%**

28. $\frac{(10^2)^3}{(10^2)^2}$

Multiply the exponents raised to a power.

$= \frac{10^6}{10^{-4}}$

Subtract the exponent in the denominator from the one in the numerator.

$= 10^{6-(-4)}$

Simplify.

$= 10^{10} =$ **10,000,000,000**

29. $\frac{(x^{-2}y^2)^2}{x^3y}$

Multiply the exponents raised to a power.

$= \frac{x^{-4}y^4}{x^3y}$

Subtract the exponent in the denominator from the one in the numerator.

$= x^{-4-3}y^{4-1} = x^{-7}y^3$

Move negative exponents to the denominator.

$= \mathbf{\frac{y^3}{x^7}}$

30. $\sqrt{48}$

Determine the largest square number that is a factor of the radicand (48) and write the radicand as a product using that square number as a factor.

$= \sqrt{16 \times 3}$

Apply the rules of radicals to simplify.

$= \sqrt{16}\sqrt{3} = \mathbf{4\sqrt{3}}$

31. $\frac{6}{\sqrt{8}}$

Apply the rules of radicals to simplify.

$= \frac{6}{\sqrt{4}\sqrt{2}} = \frac{6}{2\sqrt{2}}$

Multiply by $\frac{\sqrt{2}}{\sqrt{2}}$ to rationalize the denominator.

$= \frac{6}{2\sqrt{2}}\left(\frac{\sqrt{2}}{\sqrt{2}}\right) = \mathbf{\frac{3\sqrt{2}}{2}}$

32. 8!

Expand the factorial and multiply.

$= 8 \times 7 \times 6 \times 5 \times 4 \times 3 \times 2 \times 1$

$=$ **40,320**

33. $\frac{10!}{7!3!}$

Expand the factorial.

$= \frac{10 \times 9 \times 8 \times 7!}{7! \times 3 \times 2 \times 1}$

Cross out values that occur in both the numerator and denominator.

$= \frac{10 \times 9 \times 8}{3 \times 2 \times 1}$

Multiply and simplify.

$= \frac{720}{6} =$ **120**

34. Identify the variables given.

$a_1 = -57$

$d = -57 - (-40) = 17$

$n = 9$

Plug these values into the formula for the specific term of an arithmetic sequence.

$a_9 = -57 + 17(9 - 1)$

Solve for a_9.

$a_9 = -57 + 17(8)$

$a_9 = -57 + 136$

$\mathbf{a_9 = 79}$

35. Idenfity the variables given.

$a_5 = 200$

$a_{23} = 820$

$n = 23$

$m = 5$

$d = ?$

Plug these values into the equation for using one term to find another in an arithmetic sequence.

$a_n = a_m + d(n - m)$

$820 = 200 + d(23 - 5)$

$620 = d(18)$

$\mathbf{d = 34.\overline{44}}$

36. $\sum_{n=14}^{45} 2n + 10.$

Find the partial sum of the first 45 terms.

$a_1 = 2(1) + 10 = 12$

$n = 45$

$a_n = 2(45) + 10 = 100$

$S_n = \frac{n(a_1 + a_n)}{2} = \frac{45(12 + 100)}{2} = 2520$

Find the partial sum of the first 13 terms.

$a_1 = 2(1) + 10 = 12$

$n = 13$

$a_n = 2(13) + 10 = 36$

$S_n = \frac{n(a_1 + a_n)}{2} = \frac{13(12 + 36)}{2} = 312$

The sum of the terms between 14 and 45 will be the difference between S_{45} and S_{13}.

$S_{45} - S_{13} = 2520 - 312 =$ **2208**

37. Identify the variables given.

$a_1 = 13$

$n = 8$

$r = \frac{39}{13} = 3$

Plug these values into the equation to find a specific term in a geometric sequence.

$a_8 = 13 \times 3^{8-1}$

$a_8 = 13 \times 2187 = 28{,}431$

The eighth term of the given sequence is **28,431**.

38. Identify the variables given.

$a_1 = -4$

$n = 10$

$r = \frac{16}{-4} = -4$

Plug these values into the equation for the partial sum of a geometric sequence.

$S_{10} = \frac{-4(1-(-4)^{10})}{1-(-4)}$

$= \frac{-4(1-1{,}048{,}576)}{5} = \frac{4{,}194{,}300}{5}$

$=$ **838,860**

TEST YOUR KNOWLEDGE

1. **D) is correct.**

   Divide the digits and subtract the exponents.

   $\frac{7.2 \times 10^6}{1.6 \times 10^{-3}}$

   $7.2 \div 1.6 = 4.5$

   $6 - (-3) = 9$

   $\mathbf{4.5 \times 10^9}$

2. **D) is correct.**

   Simplify using PEMDAS.

   $(3^2 \div 1^3) - (4 - 8^2) + 2^4$

   $= (9 \div 1) - (4 - 64) + 16$

   $= 9 - (-60) + 16 = \mathbf{85}$

3. **C) is correct.**

   total seats = 4,500 + 2,000

   $\frac{\text{lower seats}}{\text{all seats}} = \frac{4{,}500}{6{,}500} = \mathbf{\frac{9}{13}}$

4. **C) is correct.**

   Use the formula for percentages.

   $\text{percent} = \frac{\text{part}}{\text{whole}}$

   $= \frac{42}{48}$

   $= 0.875 = \mathbf{87.5\%}$

5. **B) is correct.**

   Write a proportion and then solve for *x*.

   $\frac{15{,}036}{7} = \frac{x}{2}$

   $7x = 30{,}072$

   $\mathbf{x = 4{,}296}$

6. **B) is correct.**

   Use the rules of exponents to simplify the expression.

   $\frac{(3x^2y^2)^2}{3^3x^{-2}y^3} = \frac{3^2x^4y^4}{3^3x^{-2}y^3} = \mathbf{\frac{x^6y}{3}}$

7. $\mathbf{\frac{87}{19}}$ **is correct.**

   Simplify using PEMDAS.

   $\frac{5^2(3) + 3(-2)^2}{4 + 3^2 - 2(5 - 8)}$

   $= \frac{5^2(3) + 3(-2)^2}{4 + 3^2 - 2(-3)}$

   $= \frac{25(3) + 3(4)}{4 + 9 - 2(-3)}$

   $= \frac{75 + 12}{13 + 6} = \mathbf{\frac{87}{19}}$

8. **180.4 feet is correct.**

   Multiply by the converstion factor to get from meters to feet.

   $55 \text{ m} \left(\frac{3.28 \text{ ft.}}{1 \text{ m}}\right) = \mathbf{180.4 \text{ feet}}$

CHAPTER TWO
Algebra

Algebra, meaning "restoration" in Arabic, is the mathematical method of finding the unknown. The first algebraic book in Egypt was used to figure out complex inheritances that were to be split among many individuals. Today, algebra is just as necessary when dealing with unknown amounts.

Algebraic Expressions

The foundation of algebra is the **VARIABLE**, an unknown number represented by a symbol (usually a letter such as x or a). Variables can be preceded by a **COEFFICIENT**, which is a constant (i.e., a real number) in front of the variable, such as $4x$ or $-2a$. An **ALGEBRAIC EXPRESSION** is any sum, difference, product, or quotient of variables and numbers (for example $3x^2$, $2x + 7y - 1$, and $\frac{5}{x}$ are algebraic expressions). **TERMS** are any quantities that are added or subtracted (for example, the terms of the expression $x^2 - 3x + 5$ are x^2, $3x$, and 5). A **POLYNOMIAL EXPRESSION** is an algebraic expression where all the exponents on the variables are whole numbers. A polynomial with only two terms is known as a **BINOMIAL**, and one with three terms is a **TRINOMIAL**. A **MONOMIAL** has only one term.

DID YOU KNOW?
Simplified expressions are ordered by variable terms alphabetically with highest exponent first then down to constants.

EVALUATING EXPRESSIONS is another way of saying "find the numeric value of an expression if the variable is equal to a certain number." To evaluate the expression, simply plug the given value(s) for the variable(s) into the equation and simplify. Remember to use the order of operations when simplifying:

1. **P**arentheses
2. **E**xponents
3. **M**ultiplication

4. Division
5. Addition
6. Subtraction

EXAMPLE

1. If $m = 4$, find the value of the following expression: $5(m-2)^3 + 3m^2 - \frac{m}{4} - 1$

Operations with Expressions

ADDING and SUBTRACTING

Expressions can be added or subtracted by simply adding and subtracting **LIKE TERMS**, which are terms with the same variable part (the variables must be the same, with the same exponents on each variable). For example, in the expressions $2x + 3xy - 2z$ and $6y + 2xy$, the like terms are $3xy$ and $2xy$. Adding the two expressions yields the new expression $2x + 6xy - 2z + 6y$. Note that the other terms did not change; they cannot be combined because they have different variables.

EXAMPLE

2. If $a = 12x + 7xy - 9y$ and $b = 8x - 9xz + 7z$, what is $a + b$?

DISTRIBUTING and FACTORING

Distributing and factoring can be seen as two sides of the same coin. **DISTRIBUTION** multiplies each term in the first factor by each term in the second factor to get rid of parentheses. **FACTORING** reverses this process, taking a polynomial in standard form and writing it as a product of two or more factors.

DID YOU KNOW?
Operations with polynomials can always be checked by evaluating equivalent expressions for the same value.

When distributing a monomial through a polynomial, the expression outside the parentheses is multiplied by each term inside the parentheses. Using the rules of exponents, coefficients are multiplied and exponents are added.

When simplifying two polynomials, each term in the first polynomial must multiply each term in the second polynomial. A binomial (two terms) multiplied by a binomial, will require 2×2 or 4 multiplications. For the binomial × binomial case, this process is sometimes called **FOIL**, which stands for first, outside, inside, and last. These terms refer to the placement of each term of the expression: multiply the first term in each expression, then the outside terms, then the inside terms, and finally the last terms. A binomial (two terms) multiplied by a trinomial (three terms), will require 2×3 or 6 products to simplify. The first term in the first polynomial multiplies each of the three terms in the second polynomial, then the second term in the first polynomial multiplies each of the three terms in the second polynomial. A trinomial (three terms) by a trinomial will require 3×3 or 9 products, and so on.

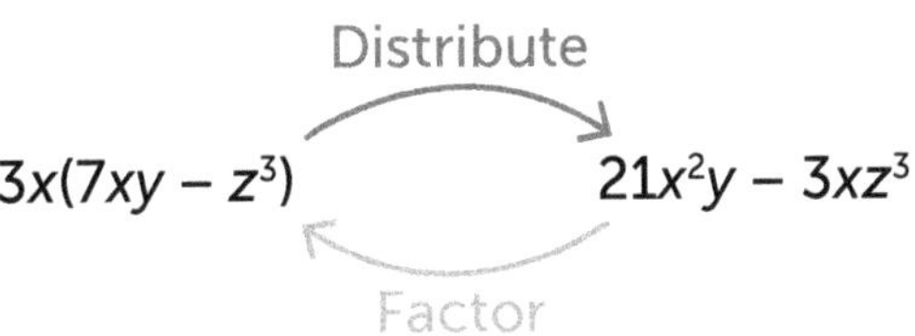

Figure 2.1. Distribution and Factoring

Factoring is the reverse of distributing: the first step is always to remove ("undistribute") the GCF of all the terms, if there is a GCF (besides 1). The GCF is the product of any constants and/or variables that <u>every</u> term shares. (For example, the GCF of $12x^3$, $15x^2$ and $6xy^2$ is $3x$ because $3x$ evenly divides all three terms.) This shared factor can be taken out of each term and moved to the outside of the parentheses, leaving behind a polynomial where each term is the original term divided by the GCF. (The remaining terms for the terms in the example would be $4x^2$, $5x$, and $2xy$.) It may be possible to factor the polynomial in the parentheses further, depending on the problem.

EXAMPLES

3. Expand the following expression: $5x(x^2 - 2c + 10)$

4. Expand the following expression: $(x^2 - 5)(2x - x^3)$

5. Factor the expression $16z^2 + 48z$

6. Factor the expression $6m^3 + 12m^3n - 9m^2$

FACTORING TRINOMIALS

If the leading coefficient is $a = 1$, the trinomial is in the form $x^2 + bx + c$ and can often be rewritten in the factored form, as a product of two binomials: $(x + m)(x + n)$. Recall that the product of two binomials can be written in expanded form $x^2 + mx + nx + mn$. Equating this expression with $x^2 + bx + c$, the constant term c would have to equal the product mn. Thus, to work backward from the trinomial to the factored form, consider all the numbers m and n that multiply to make c. For example, to factor $x^2 + 8x + 12$, consider all the pairs that multiply to be 12 ($12 = 1 \times 12$ or 2×6 or 3×4). Choose the pair that will make the coefficient of the middle term (8) when added. In this example 2 and 6 add to 8, so making $m = 2$ and $n = 6$ in the expanded form gives:

$$x^2 + 8x + 12 = x^2 + 2x + 6x + 12$$

$= (x^2 + 2x) + (6x + 12)$	Group the first two terms and the last two terms.
$= x(x + 6) + 2(x + 6)$	Factor the GCF out of each set of parentheses.
$= (x + 6)(x + 2)$	The two terms now have the common factor $(x + 6)$, which can be removed, leaving $(x + 2)$ and the original polynomial is factored.

In general:

$$x^2 + bx + c = x^2 + mx + nx + mn, \text{ where } c = mn \text{ and } b = m + n$$

$= (x^2 + mx) + (nx + mn)$	Group.
$= x(x + m) + n(x + m)$	Factor each group.
$= (x + m)(x + n)$	Factor out the common binomial.

Note that if none of the factors of c add to the value b, then the trinomial cannot be factored, and is called **PRIME.**

If the leading coefficient is not 1 ($a \neq 1$), first make sure that any common factors among the three terms are factored out. If the a-value is negative, factor out –1 first as well. If the a-value of the new polynomial in the parentheses is still not 1, follow this rule: Identify two values r and s that multiply to be ac and add to be b. Then write the polynomial in this form: $ax^2 + bx + c = ax^2 + rx + sx + c$, and proceed by grouping, factoring, and removing the common binomial as above.

There are a few special factoring cases worth memorizing: difference of squares, binomial squared, and the sum and difference of cubes.

- **DIFFERENCE OF SQUARES** (each term is a square and they are subtracted):
  - $a^2 - b^2 = (a + b)(a - b)$
  - Note that a SUM of squares is never factorable.
- **BINOMIAL SQUARED:** $a^2 + 2ab + b^2 = (a + b)(a + b) = (a + b)^2$
- **SUM AND DIFFERENCE OF CUBES:**
  - $a^3 + b^3 = (a + b)(a^2 - ab + b^2)$
  - $a^3 - b^3 = (a - b)(a^2 + ab + b^2)$
  - Note that the second factor in these factorizations will never be able to be factored further.

EXAMPLES

7. Factor: $16x^2 + 52x + 30$

8. Factor: $-21x^2 - x + 10$

Linear Equations

An **EQUATION** states that two expressions are equal to each other. Polynomial equations are categorized by the highest power of the variables they contain: the highest power of any exponent of a linear equation is 1, a quadratic equation has a variable raised to the second power, a cubic equation has a variable raised to the third power, and so on.

SOLVING LINEAR EQUATIONS

Solving an equation means finding the value or values of the variable that make the equation true. To solve a linear equation, it is necessary to manipulate the terms so that the variable being solved for appears alone on one side of the equal sign while everything else in the equation is on the other side.

The way to solve linear equations is to "undo" all the operations that connect numbers to the variable of interest. Follow these steps:

1. Eliminate fractions by multiplying each side by the least common multiple of any denominators.
2. Distribute to eliminate parentheses, braces, and brackets.
3. Combine like terms.
4. Use addition or subtraction to collect all terms containing the variable of interest to one side, and all terms not containing the variable to the other side.
5. Use multiplication or division to remove coefficients from the variable of interest.

DID YOU KNOW?

On multiple choice tests, it is often easier to plug the possible values into the equation and determine which solution makes the equation true than to solve the equation.

Sometimes there are no numeric values in the equation or there are a mix of numerous variables and constants. The goal is to solve the equation for one of the variables in terms of the other variables. In this case, the answer will be an expression involving numbers and letters instead of a numeric value.

EXAMPLES

9. Solve for x: $\frac{100(x+5)}{20} = 1$

10. Solve for x: $2(x + 2)^2 - 2x^2 + 10 = 42$

11. Solve the equation for D: $\frac{A(3B + 2D)}{2N} = 5M - 6$

GRAPHS of LINEAR EQUATIONS

The most common way to write a linear equation is **SLOPE-INTERCEPT FORM**, $y = mx + b$. In this equation, m is the slope, which describes how steep the line is, and b is the y-intercept. Slope is often described as "rise over run" because it is calculated as the difference in y-values (rise) over the difference in x-values (run). The slope of the line is also the rate of change of the dependent variable y with respect to the independent variable x. The y-intercept is the point where the line crosses the y-axis, or where x equals zero.

DID YOU KNOW?

Use the phrase "Begin, Move" to remember that b is the y-intercept (where to begin) and m is the slope (how the line moves).

To graph a linear equation, identify the y-intercept and place that point on the y-axis. If the slope is not written as a fraction, make it a fraction by writing it over 1 $\left(\frac{m}{1}\right)$. Then use the slope to count up (or down, if negative) the "rise" part of the slope and over the "run" part of the slope to find a second point. These points can then be connected to draw the line.

To find the equation of a line, identify the y-intercept, if possible, on the graph and use two easily identifiable points to find the slope. If the y-intercept is not easily identified, identify the slope by choosing easily identifiable points; then choose one point on the graph, plug the point and the slope values into the equation, and solve for the missing value b.

- standard form: $Ax + By = C$
- $m = -\frac{A}{B}$
- x-intercept $= \frac{C}{A}$
- y-intercept $= \frac{C}{B}$

Another way to express a linear equation is standard form: $Ax + By = C$. In order to graph equations in this form, it is often easiest to convert them to point-slope form. Alternately, it is easy to find the x- or y-intercept from this form, and once these two points are known, a line can be drawn through them. To find the x-intercept, simply make $y = 0$ and solve for x. Similarly, to find the y-intercept, make $x = 0$ and solve for y.

DID YOU KNOW?

slope-intercept form:
$y = mx + b$
slope: $m = \frac{y_2 - y_1}{x_2 - x_1}$

EXAMPLES

12. What is the slope of the line whose equation is $6x - 2y - 8 = 0$?

13. Write the equation of the line which passes through the points (–2,5) and (–5,3).

14. What is the equation of the following line?

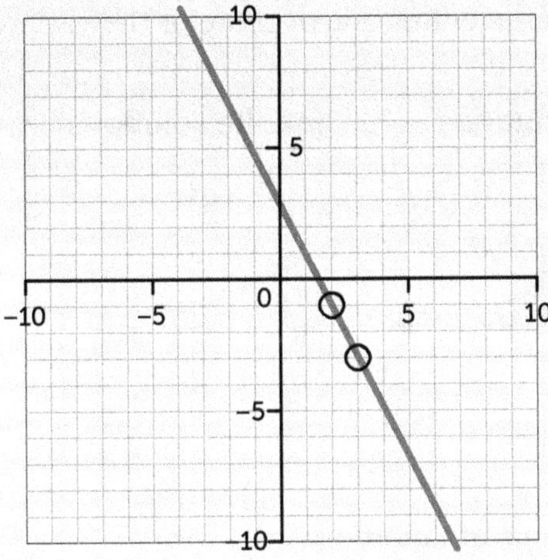

15. What is the equation of the following graph?

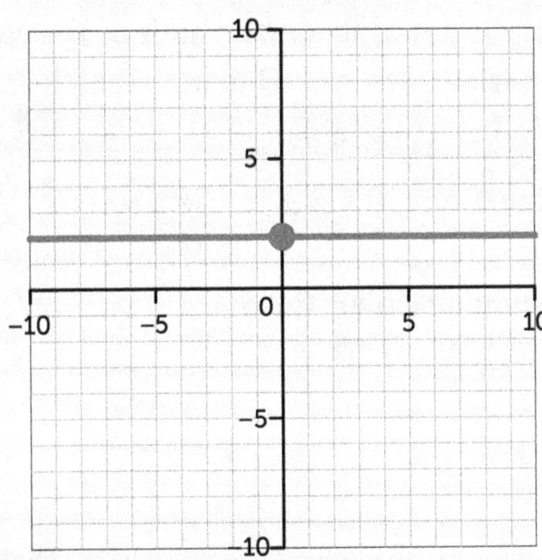

SYSTEMS of LINEAR EQUATIONS

Systems of equations are sets of equations that include two or more variables. These systems can only be solved when there are at least as many equations as there are variables. Systems involve working with more than one equation to solve for more than one variable. For a system of linear equations, the solution to the system is the set of values for the variables that satisfies every equation in the system. Graphically, this will be the point where every line meets. If the lines are parallel (and hence do not intersect), the system will have no solution. If the lines are multiples of each other, meaning they share all coordinates, then the system has infinitely many solutions (because every point on the line is a solution).

DID YOU KNOW?
Plug answers back into both equations to ensure the system has been solved properly.

There are three common methods for solving systems of equations. To perform **SUBSTITUTION**, solve one equation for one variable, and then plug in the resulting expression for that variable in the second equation. This process works best for systems of two equations with two variables where the coefficient of one or more of the variables is 1.

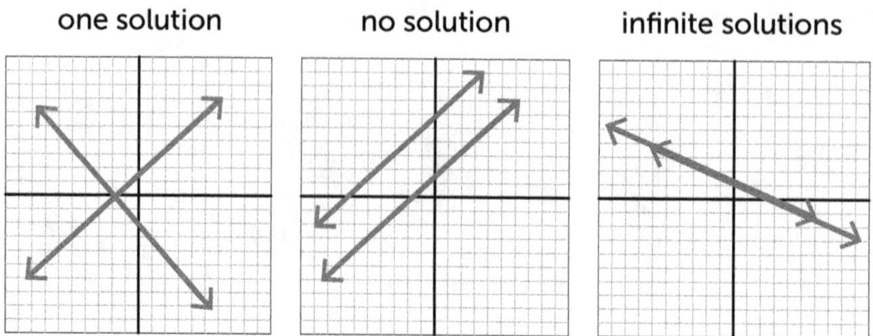

Figure 2.2. Systems of Equations

To solve using **ELIMINATION**, add or subtract two equations so that one or more variables are eliminated. It's often necessary to multiply one or both of the equations by a scalar (constant) in order to make the variables cancel. Equations can be added or subtracted as many times as necessary to find each variable.

Yet another way to solve a system of linear equations is to use a **MATRIX EQUATION**. In the matrix equation $AX = B$, A contains the system's coefficients, X contains the variables, and B contains the constants (as shown below). The matrix equation can then be solved by multiplying B by the inverse of A: $\boldsymbol{X = A^{-1}B}$

$$\begin{matrix} ax + by = e \\ cx + dy = f \end{matrix} \rightarrow A = \begin{bmatrix} a & b \\ c & d \end{bmatrix} \; X = \begin{bmatrix} x \\ y \end{bmatrix} \; B = \begin{bmatrix} e \\ f \end{bmatrix} \rightarrow AX = B$$

This method can be extended to equations with three or more variables. Technology (such as a graphing calculator) is often employed when solving using this method if more than two variables are involved.

EXAMPLES

16. Solve for x and y:

$2x - 4y = 28$

$4x - 12y = 36$

17. Solve for the system for x and y:

$3 = -4x + y$

$16x = 4y + 2$

18. Solve the system of equations:

$6x + 10y = 18$

$4x + 15y = 37$

19. Solve the following systems of equations using matrix arithmetic:

$2x - 3y = -5$

$3x - 4y = -8$

BUILDING EQUATIONS

In word problems, it is often necessary to translate a verbal description of a relationship into a mathematical equation. No matter the problem, this process can be done using the same steps:

1. Read the problem carefully and identify what value needs to be solved for.
2. Identify the known and unknown quantities in the problem, and assign the unknown quantities a variable.
3. Create equations using the variables and known quantities.
4. Solve the equations.
5. Check the solution: Does it answer the question asked in the problem? Does it make sense?

EXAMPLES

20. A school is holding a raffle to raise money. There is a $3 entry fee, and each ticket costs $5. If a student paid $28, how many tickets did he buy?

21. Kelly is selling shirts for her school swim team. There are two prices: a student price and a nonstudent price. During the first week of the sale, Kelly raised $84 by selling 10 shirts to students and 4 shirts to nonstudents. She earned $185 in the second week by selling 20 shirts to students and 10 shirts to nonstudents. What is the student price for a shirt?

Linear Inequalities

SOLVING LINEAR INEQUALITIES

An inequality shows the relationship between two expressions, much like an equation. However, the equal sign is replaced with an inequality symbol that expresses the following relationships:

- $<$ less than
- $>$ greater than
- $\leq$ less than or equal to
- $\geq$ greater than or equal to

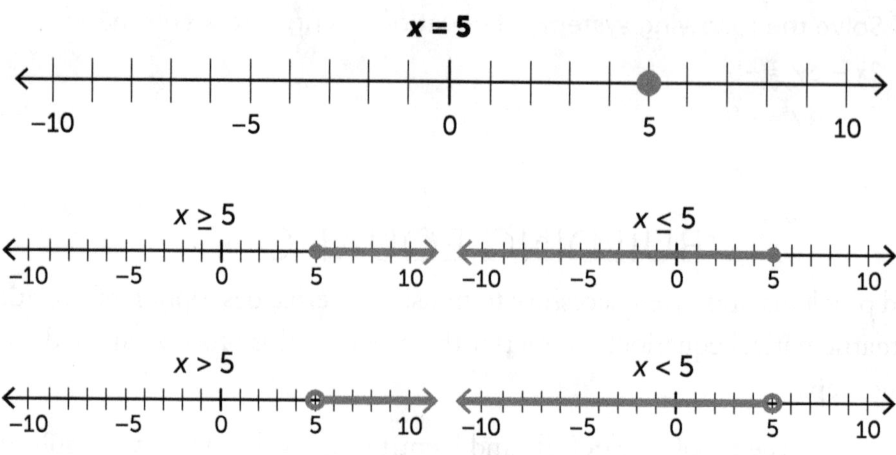

Figure 2.3. Inequalities on a Number Line

Inequalities are read from left to right. For example, the inequality $x \leq 8$ would be read as "x is less than or equal to 8," meaning x has a value smaller than or equal to 8. The set of solutions of an inequality can be expressed using a number line. The shaded region on the number line represents the set of all the numbers that make an inequality true. One major difference between equations and inequalities is that equations generally have a finite number of solutions, while inequalities generally have infinitely many solutions (an entire interval on the number line containing infinitely many values).

Linear inequalities can be solved in the same way as linear equations, with one exception. When multiplying or dividing both sides of an inequality by a negative number, the direction of the inequality sign must reverse—"greater than" becomes "less than" and "less than" becomes "greater than."

EXAMPLES

22. Solve for z: $3z + 10 < -z$

23. Solve for x: $2x - 3 > 5(x - 4) - (x - 4)$

COMPOUND INEQUALITIES

Compound inequalities have more than one inequality expression. Solutions of compound inequalities are the sets of all numbers that make *all* the inequalities true. Some compound inequalities may not have any solutions, some will have solutions that contain some part of the number line, and some will have solutions that include the entire number line.

Compound inequalities can be written, solved, and graphed as two separate inequalities. For compound inequalities in which the word *and* is used, the solution to the compound inequality will be the set of numbers on the number line where both inequalities have solutions (where both are shaded). For compound inequalities where *or* is used, the solution to the compound inequality will be *all* the shaded regions for *either* inequality.

Table 2.1. Unions and Intersections

Inequality	Meaning in Words	Number Line
$a < x < b$	All values x that are greater than a and less than b	a b
$a \leq x \leq b$	All values x that are greater than or equal to a and less than or equal to b	a b
$x < a$ or $x > b$	All values of x that are less than a or greater than b	a b
$x \leq a$ or $x \geq b$	All values of x that are less than or equal to a or greater than or equal to b	a b

EXAMPLES

24. Solve the compound inequalities: $2x + 4 < -18$ *or* $4(x + 2) > 18$

25. Solve the inequality: $-1 \leq 3(x + 2) - 1 \leq x + 3$

GRAPHING LINEAR INEQUALITIES in TWO VARIABLES

Linear inequalities in two variables can be graphed in much the same way as linear equations. Start by graphing the corresponding equation of a line (temporarily replace the inequality with an equal sign, and then graph). This line creates a boundary line of two half-planes. If the inequality is a "greater/less than," the boundary should not be included and a dotted line is used. A solid line is used to indicate that the boundary should be included in the solution when the inequality is "greater/less than or equal to."

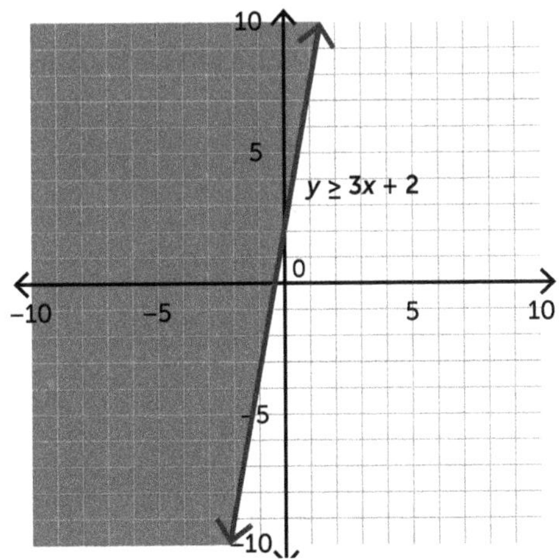

Figure 2.4. Graphing Inequalities

One side of the boundary is the set of all points (x, y) that make the inequality true. This side is shaded to indicate that all these values are solutions. If y is greater than the expression containing x, shade above the line; if it is less than, shade below. A point can also be used to check which side of the line to shade.

DID YOU KNOW?

A dotted line is used for "greater/less than" because the solution may approach that line, but the coordinates on the line can never be a solution.

A set of two or more linear inequalities is a **SYSTEM OF INEQUALITIES.** Solutions to the system are all the values of the variables that make every inequality in the system true. Systems of inequalities are solved graphically by graphing all the inequalities in the same plane. The region where all the shaded solutions overlap is the solution to the system.

EXAMPLES

26. Graph the following inequality: $3x + 6y \leq 12$.

27. Graph the system of inequalities: $-x + y \leq 1, x \geq -1, y > 2x - 4$

28. What is the inequality represented on the graph below?

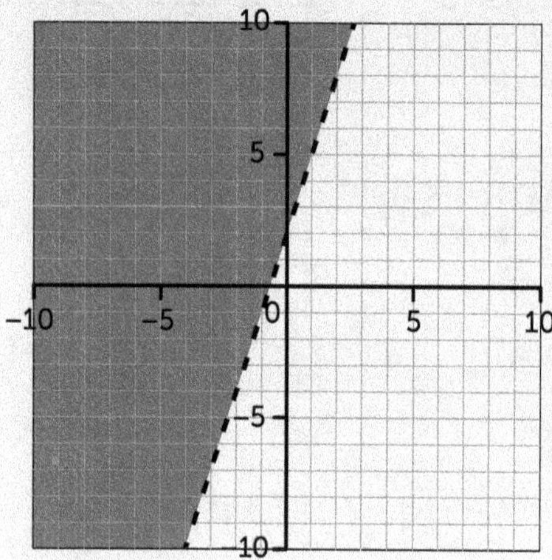

Quadratic Equations and Inequalities

Quadratic equations are degree 2 polynomials; the highest power on the dependent variable is two. While linear functions are represented graphically as lines, the graph of a quadratic function is a **PARABOLA.** The graph of a parabola has three important components. The **VERTEX** is where the graph changes direction. In the parent graph $y = x^2$, the origin $(0, 0)$ is the vertex. The **AXIS OF SYMMETRY** is the vertical line that cuts the graph into two equal halves. The line of symmetry always passes through the vertex. On the parent graph, the y-axis is the axis of symmetry. The **ZEROS** or **ROOTS** of the quadratic are the x-intercepts of the graph.

FORMS of QUADRATIC EQUATIONS

Quadratic equations can be expressed in two forms:

- **STANDARD FORM:** $y = ax^2 + bx + c$
  - Axis of symmetry: $x = -\frac{b}{2a}$
  - Vertex: $(-\frac{b}{2a}, f(-\frac{b}{2a}))$

- **VERTEX FORM:** $y \; a(x - h)^2 + k$
  - Vertex: (h, k)
  - Axis of symmetry: $x = h$

In both equations, the sign of a determines which direction the parabola opens: if a is positive, then it opens upward; if a is negative, then it opens downward. The wideness or narrowness is also determined by a. If the absolute value of a is less than one (a proper fraction), then the parabola will get wider the closer $|a|$ is to zero. If the absolute value of a is greater than one, then the larger $|a|$ becomes, the narrower the parabola will be.

Equations in vertex form can be converted to standard form by squaring out the $(x - h)^2$ part (using FOIL), distributing the a, adding k, and simplifying the result.

Equations can be converted from standard form to vertex form by **COMPLETING THE SQUARE.** Take an equation in standard form, $y = ax^2 + bc + c$.

1. Move c to the left side of the equation.
2. Divide the entire equation through by a (to make the coefficient of x^2 be 1).
3. Take half of the coefficient of x, square that number, and then add the result to both sides of the equation.
4. Convert the right side of the equation to a perfect binomial squared, $(x + m)^2$.
5. Isolate y to put the equation in proper vertex form.

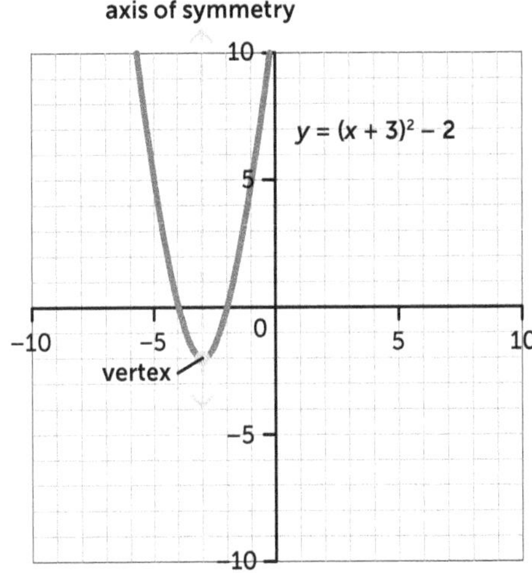

Figure 2.5. Parabola

EXAMPLES

29. What is the line of symmetry for $y = -2(x + 3)^2 + 2$?

30. What is the vertex of the parabola $y = -3x^2 + 24x - 27$?

31. Write $y = -3x^2 + 24x - 27$ in vertex form by completing the square.

SOLVING QUADRATIC EQUATIONS

Solving the quadratic equation $ax^2 + bx + c = 0$ finds x-intercepts of the parabola (by making $y = 0$). These are also called the **ROOTS** or **ZEROS** of the quadratic function. A quadratic equation may have zero, one, or two real solutions. There are several ways of finding the zeros. One way is to factor the quadratic into a product of two binomials, and then use the zero product property. (If $m \times n = 0$, then either $m = 0$ or $n = 0$.)

Another way is to complete the square and square root both sides. One way that works every time is to memorize and use the **QUADRATIC FORMULA:**

DID YOU KNOW?

With all graphing problems, putting the function into the $y =$ window of a graphing calculator will aid the process of elimination when graphs are examined and compared to answer choices with a focus on properties like axis of symmetry, vertices, and roots of formulas.

$$x = \frac{-b \pm \sqrt{b^2 - 4ac}}{2a}$$

The a, b, and c come from the standard form of quadratic equations above. (Note that to use the quadratic equation, the right-hand side of the equation must be equal to zero.)

The part of the formula under the square root radical ($b^2 - 4ac$) is known as the **DISCRIMINANT**. The discriminant tells how many and what type of roots will result without actually calculating the roots.

Table 2.2. Discriminants

If $b^2 - 4ac$ is	There will be	And the parabola
zero	only 1 real root	has its vertex on the x-axis
positive	2 real roots	has two x-intercepts
negative	0 real roots 2 complex roots	has no x-intercepts

EXAMPLES

32. Find the zeros of the quadratic equation: $y = -(x + 3)^2 + 1$.

33. Find the root(s) for: $z^2 - 4z + 4 = 0$

34. Write a quadratic function that has zeros at $x = -3$ and $x = 2$ that passes through the point $(-2,8)$.

GRAPHING QUADRATIC EQUATIONS

The final expected quadratic skills are graphing a quadratic function given its equation and determining the equation of a quadratic function from its graph. The equation's form determines which quantities are easiest to obtain:

To graph a quadratic function, first determine if the graph opens up or down by examining the a-value. Then determine the quantity that is easiest to find based on the form given, and find the vertex. Then other values can be found, if necessary, by choosing x-values and finding the corresponding y-values. Using symmetry instantly doubles the number of points that are known.

Table 2.3. Obtaining Quantities from Quadratic Functions			
Name of Form	**Equation of Quadratic**	**Easiest Quantity to Find**	**How to Find Other Quantities**
vertex form	$y = a(x - h)^2 + k$	vertex at (h,k) and axis of symmetry $x = h$	Find zeros by making $y = 0$ and solving for x.
factored form	$y = a(x - m)(x - n)$	x – intercepts at $x = m$ and $x = n$	Find axis of symmetry by averaging m and n: $x = \frac{m+n}{2}$. This is also the x-value of the vertex.
standard form	$y = ax^2 + bx + c$	y–intercept at $(0,c)$	Find axis of symmetry and x-value of the vertex using $x = \frac{-b}{2a}$. Find zeros using quadratic formula.

Given the graph of a parabola, the easiest way to write a quadratic equation is to identify the vertex and insert the h- and k-values into the vertex form of the equation. The a-value can be determined by finding another point the graph goes through, plugging these values in for x and y, and solving for a.

EXAMPLES

35. Graph the quadratic $y = 2(x - 3)^2 + 4$.

36. What is the vertex form of the equation shown on the following graph?

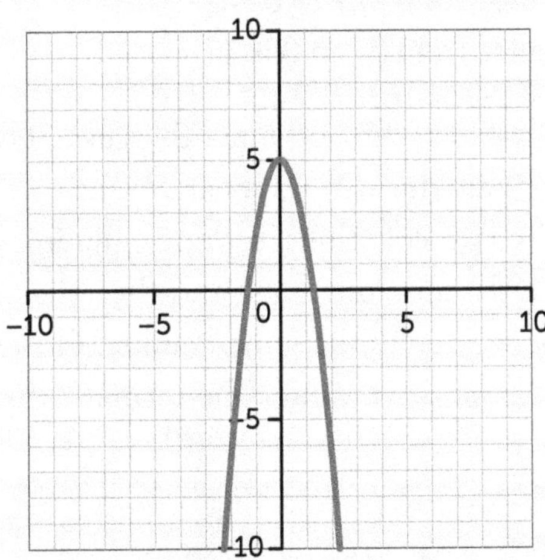

QUADRATIC INEQUALITIES

Quadratic inequalities with two variables, such as $y < (x + 3)^2 - 2$ can be graphed much like linear inequalities: graph the equation by treating the inequality symbol as

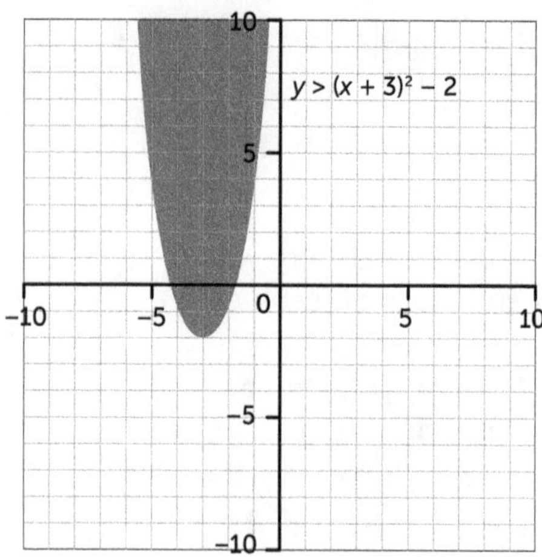

Figure 2.6. Quadratic Inequality

an equal sign, then shade the graph. Shade above the graph when y is greater is than, and below the graph when y is less than.

Quadratic inequalities with only one variable, such as $x^2 - 4x > 12$, can be solved by first manipulating the inequality so that one side is zero. The zeros can then be found and used to determine where the inequality is greater than zero (positive) or less than zero (negative). Often it helps to set up intervals on a number line and test a value within each range created by the zeros to identify the values that create positive or negative values.

EXAMPLE

37. Find the values of x such that $x^2 - 4x > 12$.

Absolute Value Equations and Inequalities

The **ABSOLUTE VALUE** of a number means the distance between that number and zero. The absolute value of any number is positive since distance is always positive. The notation for absolute value of a number is two vertical bars:

$\lvert -27 \rvert = 27$	The distance from −27 to 0 is 27.
$\lvert 27 \rvert = 27$	The distance from 27 to 0 is 27.

Solving equations and simplifying inequalities with absolute values usually requires writing two equations or inequalities, which are then solved separately using the usual methods of solving equations. To write the two equations, set one equation equal to the positive value of the expression inside the absolute value and the other equal to the negative value. Two inequalities can be written in the same manner. However, the inequality symbol should be flipped for the negative value. The formal definition of the absolute value is

$$|x| = \begin{cases} -x, & x < 0 \\ x, & x \geq 0 \end{cases}$$

This is true because whenever x is negative, the opposite of x is the answer (for example, $|-5| = -(-5) = 5$, but when x is positive, the answer is just x. This type of function is called a **PIECE-WISE FUNCTION**. It is defined in two (or more) distinct pieces. To graph the absolute value function, graph each piece separately. When $x < 0$ (that is, when it is negative), graph the line $y = -x$. When $x > 0$ (that is, when x is positive), graph the line $y = x$. This creates a V-shaped graph that is the parent function for absolute value functions.

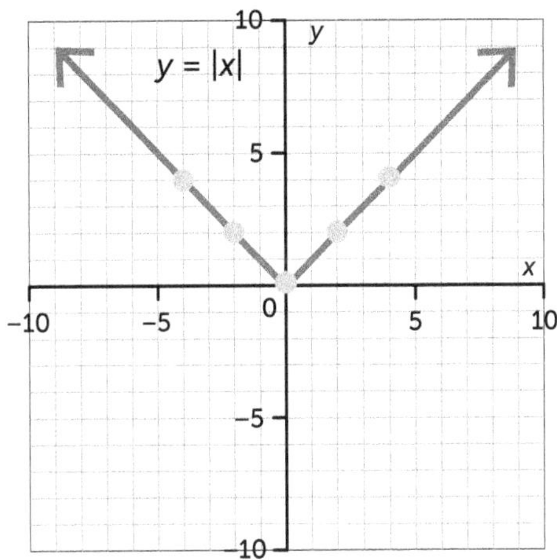

Figure 2.7. Absolute Value Parent Function

EXAMPLES

38. Solve for x: $|x - 3| = 27$

39. Solve for r: $\frac{|r-7|}{5} = 27$

40. Find the solution set for the following inequality: $\left|\frac{3x}{7}\right| \geq 4 - x$.

Functions

WORKING with FUNCTIONS

Functions can be thought of as a process: when something is put in, an action (or operation) is performed, and something different comes out. A **FUNCTION** is a relationship between two quantities (for example x and y) in which, for every value of the independent variable (usually x), there is exactly one value of the dependent variable (usually y). Briefly, each input has *exactly one* output. Graphically this means the graph passes the **VERTICAL LINE TEST**: anywhere a vertical line is drawn on the graph, the line hits the curve at exactly one point.

The notation $f(x)$ or $g(t)$, etc., is often used when a function is being considered. This is **FUNCTION NOTATION.** The input value is x and the output value y is written as $y = f(x)$. Thus, $f(2)$ represents the output value (or y value) when $x = 2$, and $f(2) = 5$ means that when $x = 2$ is plugged into the $f(x)$ function, the output (y value) is 5. In other words, $f(2) = 5$ represents the point $(2,5)$ on the graph of $f(x)$.

Every function has an **INPUT DOMAIN** and **OUTPUT RANGE.** The domain is the set of all the possible x values that can be used as input values (these are found along the horizontal axis on the graph), and the range includes all the y values or output values that result from applying $f(x)$ (these are found along the vertical axis on the graph). Domain and range are usually intervals of numbers and are often expressed as inequalities, such as $x < 2$ (the domain is all values less than 2) or $3 < x < 15$ (all values between 3 and 15).

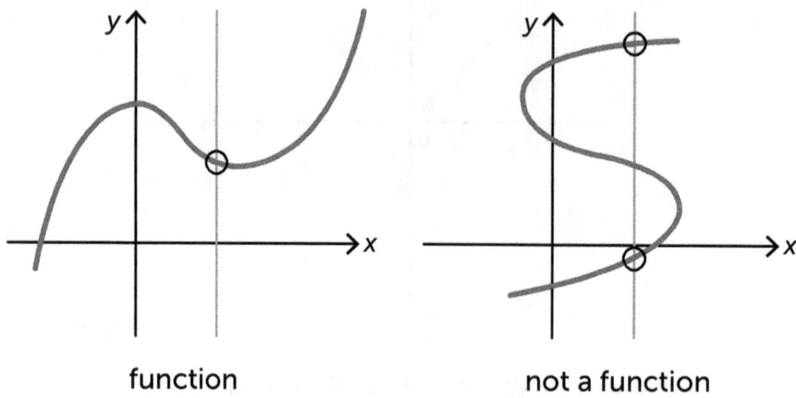

Figure 2.8. Vertical Line Test

A function $f(x)$ is **EVEN** if $f(-x) = f(x)$. Even functions have symmetry across the y-axis. An example of an even function is the parent quadratic $y = x^2$, because any value of x (for example, 3) and its opposite $-x$ (for example, -3) have the same y value (for example, $3^2 = 9$ and $(-3)^2 = 9$). A function is **ODD** if $f(-x) = -f(x)$. Odd functions have symmetry about the origin. For example, $f(x) = x^3$ is an odd function because $f(3) = 27$, and $f(-3) = -27$. A function may be even, odd, or neither.

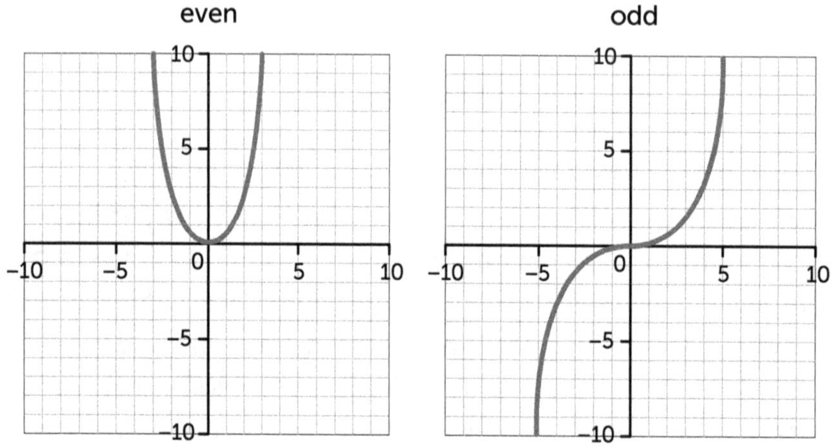

Figure 2.9. Even and Odd Functions

EXAMPLES

41. Evaluate: $f(4)$ if $f(x) = x^3 - 2x + \sqrt{x}$

42. What are the domain and range of the following function?

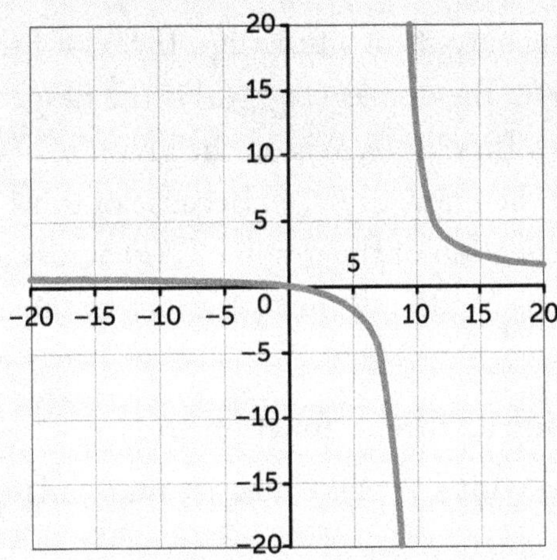

43. What is the domain and the range of the following graph?

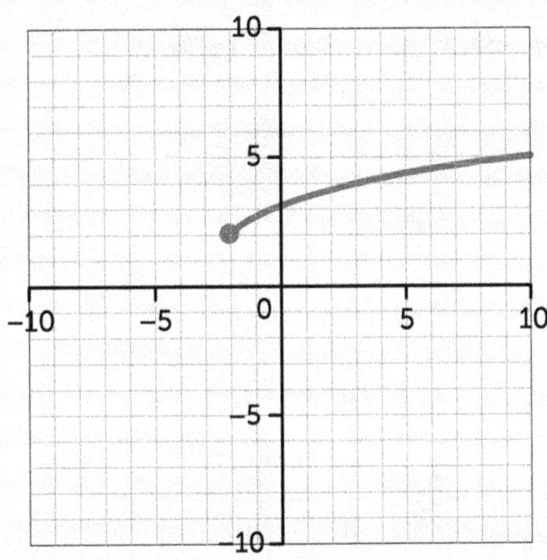

44. Which of the following represents a function?

A)

x	g(x)
0	0
1	1
2	2
1	3

B)

x	f(x)
0	1
0	2
0	3
0	4

C)

t	f(t)
1	1
2	2
3	3
4	4

D)

x	f(x)
0	0
5	1
0	2
5	3

INVERSE FUNCTIONS

Inverse functions switch the inputs and the outputs of a function. If $f(x) = k$ then the inverse of that function would read $f^{-1}(k) = x$. The domain of $f^{-1}(x)$ is the range of $f(x)$, and the range of $f^{-1}(x)$ is the domain of $f(x)$. If point (a, b) is on the graph of $f(x)$, then point (b, a) will be on the graph of $f^{-1}(x)$. Because of this fact, the graph of $f^{-1}(x)$ is a reflection of the graph of $f(x)$ across the line $y = x$. Inverse functions "undo" all the operations of the original function.

DID YOU KNOW?

Inverse graphs can be tested by taking any point on one graph and flipping coordinates to see if that new point is on the other curve. For example, the coordinate point (5,–2) is on the function and (–2,5) is a point on its inverse.

The steps for finding an inverse function are:

1. Replace $f(x)$ with y to make it easier manipulate the equation.
2. Switch the x and y.
3. Solve for y.
4. Label the inverse function as $f^{-1}(x) =$.

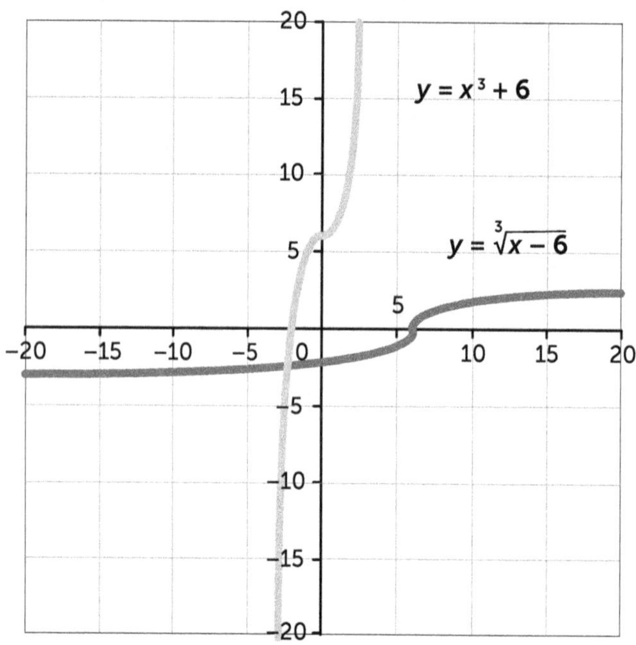

Figure 2.10. Inverse Functions

EXAMPLES

45. What is the inverse of function of $f(x) = 5x + 5$?

46. Find the inverse of the graph of $f(x) = -1 - \frac{1}{5}x$.

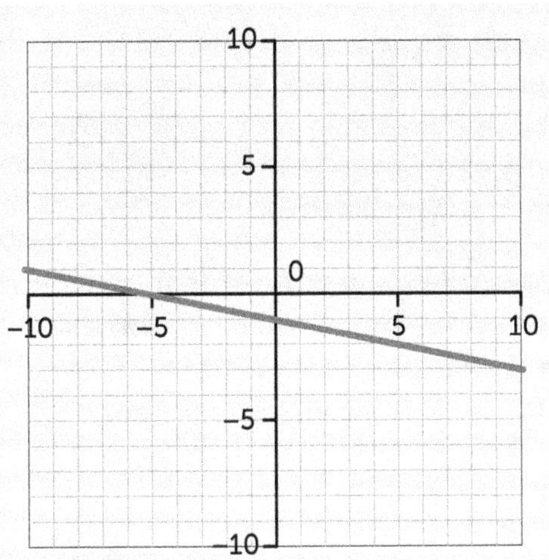

COMPOUND FUNCTIONS

COMPOUND FUNCTIONS take two or more functions and combine them using operations or composition. Functions can be combined using addition, subtraction, multiplication, or division:

- addition: $(f+g)(x) = f(x) + g(x)$
- subtraction: $(f-g)(x) = f(x) - g(x)$
- multiplication: $(fg)(x) = f(x)g(x)$
- division: $\left(\frac{f}{g}\right)(x) = \frac{f(x)}{g(x)}$ (note that $g(x) \neq 0$)

Functions can also be combined using **COMPOSITION.** Composition of functions is indicated by the notation $(f \circ g)(x)$. Note that the $\circ$ symbol does NOT mean multiply. It means take the output of $g(x)$ and make it the input of $f(x)$:

$$(f \circ g)(x) = f(g(x))$$

This equation is read f of g of x, and will be a new function of x. Note that order is important. In general, $f(g(x)) \neq g(f(x))$. They *will* be equal when $f(x)$ and $g(x)$ are inverses of each other, however, as both will simplify to the original input x. This is because performing a function on a value and then using that output as the input to the inverse function should bring you back to the original value.

The domain of a composition function is the set of x values that are in the domain of the "inside" function $g(x)$ such that $g(x)$ is in the domain of the outside function $f(x)$. For example, if $f(x) = \frac{1}{x}$ and $g(x) = \sqrt{x}$, $f(g(x))$ has a domain of $x > 0$ because $g(x)$ has a domain of $x \geq 0$. But when $f(x)$ is applied to the $\sqrt{x}$ function, the composition function becomes $\frac{1}{\sqrt{x}}$ and the value $x = 0$ is no longer allowed because it would result in 0 in the denominator, so the domain must be further restricted.

EXAMPLES

47. If $z(x) = 3x - 3$ and $y(x) = 2x - 1$, find $(y \circ z)(-4)$.

48. Find $(k \circ t)(x)$ if $k(x) = \frac{1}{2}x - 3$ and $t(x) = \frac{1}{2}x - 2$.

49. The wait (W) (in minutes) to get on a ride at an amusement park depends on the number of people (N) in the park. The number of people in the park depends on the number of hours, t, that the park has been open. Suppose $N(t) = 400t$ and $W(N) = 5(1.2)\frac{N}{100}$. What is the value and the meaning in context of $N(4)$ and $W(N(4))$?

TRANSFORMING FUNCTIONS

Many functions can be graphed using simple transformation of parent functions. Transformations include reflections across axes, vertical and horizontal translations (or shifts), and vertical or horizontal stretches or compressions. The table gives the effect of each transformation to the graph of any function $y = f(x)$.

Table 2.4. Effects of Transformations

EQUATION	EFFECT ON GRAPH
$y = -f(x)$	reflection acro50 the x-axis (vertical reflection)
$y = f(x) + k$	vertical shift up k units ($k > 0$) or down k units ($k < 0$)
$y = kf(x)$	vertical stretch (if $k > 1$) or compression (if $k < 1$)
$y = f(-x)$	reflection across the y-axis (horizontal reflection)
$y = f(x + k)$	horizontal shift right k units ($k < 0$) or left k units ($k > 0$)
$y = f(kx)$	horizontal stretch ($k < 1$) or compression ($k > 1$)

Note that the first three equations have an operation applied to the *outside* of the function $f(x)$ and these all cause *vertical changes* to the graph of the function that are **INTUITIVE** (for example, adding a value moves it up). The last three equations have an operation applied to the *inside* of the function $f(x)$ and these all cause **HORIZONTAL CHANGES** to the graph of the function that are **COUNTERINTUITIVE** (for example, multiplying the x's by a fraction results in stretch, not compression, which would seem more intuitive). It is helpful to group these patterns together to remember how each transformation affects the graph.

EXAMPLES

50. Graph: $y = |x + 1| + 4$

51. Graph: $y = -3|x - 2| + 2$

Polynomial Functions

A polynomial is any equation or expression with two or more terms with whole number exponents. All polynomials with only one variable are functions. The zeros, or roots, of a polynomial function are where the function equals zero and crosses the x-axis.

> **DID YOU KNOW?**
> All polynomials where n is an odd number will have at least one real zero or root. Complex zeros always come in pairs (specifically, complex conjugate pairs).

A linear function is a degree 1 polynomial and always has one zero. A quadratic function is a degree 2 polynomial and always has exactly two roots (including complex roots and counting repeated roots separately). This pattern is extended in the **FUNDAMENTAL THEOREM OF ALGEBRA:**

A polynomial function with degree $n > 0$ such as $f(x) = ax^n + bx^{n-1} + cx^{n-2} + \ldots + k$, has exactly n (real or complex) roots (some roots may be repeated). Simply stated, whatever the degree of the polynomial is, that is how many roots it will have.

Table 2.5. Zeros of Polynomial Functions

POLYNOMIAL DEGREE, N	NUMBER AND POSSIBLE TYPES OF ZEROS
1	1 real zero (guaranteed)
2	0, 1, or 2 real zeros possible 2 real *or* complex zeros (guaranteed)
3	1, 2, or 3 real zeros possible (there must be at least one real zero) Or 1 real zero (guaranteed) and 2 complex zeros (guaranteed)
4	0, 1, 2, 3, or 4 real zeros (possible) Or 2 real zeros and 2 complex zeros or 4 complex zeros
...	...

All the zeros of a polynomial satisfy the equation $f(x) = 0$. That is, if k is a zero of a polynomial, then plugging in $x = k$ into the polynomial results in 0. This also means that the polynomial is evenly divisible by the factor $(x - k)$.

EXAMPLE

52. Find the roots of the polynomial: $y = 3t^4 - 48$

Rational Functions

WORKING with RATIONAL FUNCTIONS

Rational functions are ratios of polynomial functions in the form $f(x) = \frac{g(x)}{h(x)}$. Just like rational numbers, rational functions form a closed system under addition, subtraction, multiplication, and division by a nonzero rational expression. This means adding two rational functions, for example, results in another rational function.

To add or subtract rational expressions, the least common denominator of the factors in the denominator must be found. Then, numerators are added, just like adding rational numbers. To multiply rational expressions, factors can be multiplied straight across, canceling factors that appear in the numerator and denominator. To divide rational functions, use the "invert and multiply" rule.

Rational equations are solved by multiplying through the equation by the least common denominator of factors in the denominator. Just like with radical equations, this process can result in extraneous solutions, so all answers need to be checked by plugging them into the original equation.

EXAMPLES

53. If $f(x) = \frac{2}{3x^2y}$ and $g(x) = \frac{5}{21y}$, find the difference between the functions, $f(x) - g(x)$.

54. If $f(x) = \frac{(x-1)(x+2)^2}{5x^2+10x}$ and $g(x) = \frac{x^2+x-2}{x+5}$, find the quotient $\frac{f(x)}{g(x)}$.

55. Solve the rational equation $\frac{x}{x+2} + \frac{2}{x^2+5x+6} = \frac{5}{x+3}$.

GRAPHING RATIONAL FUNCTIONS

Rational functions are graphed by examining the function to find key features of the graph, including asymptotes, intercepts, and holes.

A **VERTICAL ASYMPTOTE** exists at any value that makes the denominator of a (simplified) rational function equal zero. A vertical asymptote is a vertical line through an x value that is not in the domain of the rational function (the function is undefined at this value because division by 0 is not allowed). The function approaches, but never crosses, this line, and the y values increase (or decrease) without bound (or "go to infinity") as this x value is approached.

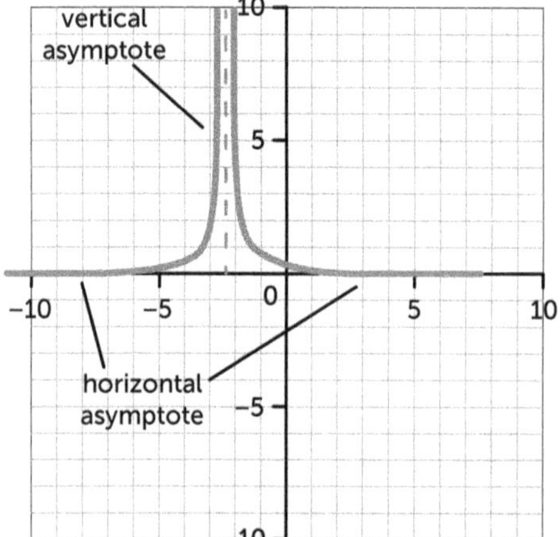

Figure 2.11. Graphing Rational Functions

To find x-intercepts and vertical asymptotes, factor the numerator and denominator of the function. Cancel any terms that appear in the numerator and denominator (if there are any). These values will appear as **HOLES** on the final graph. Since a fraction only equals 0 when its numerator is 0, set the simplified numerator equal to 0 and solve to find the x-intercepts. Next, set the denominator equal to 0 and solve to find the vertical asymptotes.

HORIZONTAL ASYMPTOTES are horizontal lines that describe the "end behavior" of a rational function. In other words, the horizontal asymptote describes what happens to the y-values of the function as the x-values get very large ($x \to \infty$) or very small ($x \to -\infty$). A horizontal asymptote occurs if the degree of the numerator of a rational function is less than or equal to the degree in the denominator. The table summarizes the conditions for horizontal asymptotes:

Table 2.6. Conditions for Horizontal Asymptotes

For polynomials with first terms $\frac{ax^n}{bx^d}$ ...		
$n < d$	as $x \to \infty, y \to 0$ as $x \to -\infty, y \to 0$	The x-axis ($y = 0$) is a horizontal asymptote.
$n = d$	as $x \to \pm\infty, y \to \frac{a}{b}$	There is a horizontal asymptote at $y = \frac{a}{b}$.
$n > d$	as $x \to \infty, y \to \infty$ or $-\infty$ as $x \to -\infty, y \to \infty$ or $-\infty$	There is no horizontal asymptote.

EXAMPLES

56. Create a function that has an x-intercept at (5, 0) and vertical asymptotes at $x = 1$ and $x = -1$.

57. Graph the function: $f(x) = \frac{3x^2 - 12x}{x^2 - 2x - 3}$.

Radical Functions

RADICAL FUNCTIONS have rational (fractional) exponents, or include the radical symbol. For example, $f(x) = 2(x - 5)^{\frac{1}{3}}$ and $g(t) = \sqrt[4]{5 - x}$ are radical functions. The domain of even root parent functions is $0 \le x \le \infty$ and the range is $y \ge 0$. For odd root parent functions, the domain is all real numbers (because you can take cube roots, etc., of negative numbers). The range is also all real numbers.

To solve equations involving radical functions, first isolate the radical part of the expression. Then "undo" the fractional exponent by raising both sides to the reciprocal of the fractional exponent (for example, undo square roots by squaring both sides). Then solve the equation using inverse operations, as always. All answers should be checked by plugging them back into the original equation, as **EXTRANEOUS SOLUTIONS** result when an equation is raised to powers on both sides. This means there may be some answers that are not actually solutions, and should be eliminated.

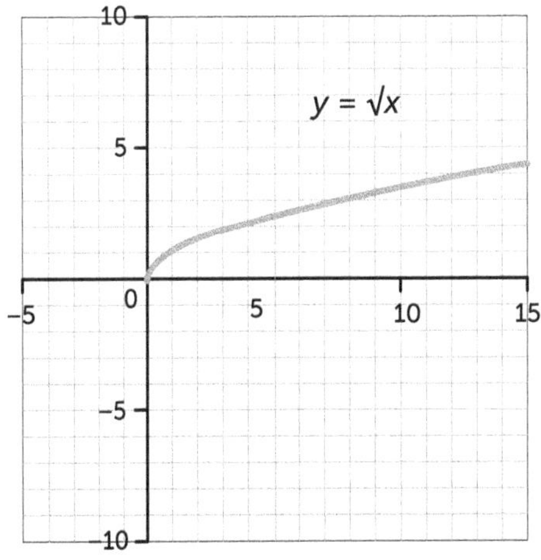

Figure 2.12. Radical Parent Function

EXAMPLES

58. Solve the equation: $\sqrt{2x-5}+4=x$

59. Solve the equation: $2(x^2-7x)^{\frac{2}{3}}=8$

Exponential and Logarithmic Functions

EXPONENTIAL FUNCTIONS

An **EXPONENTIAL FUNCTION** has a constant base and a variable in the exponent: $f(x) = b^x$ is an exponential function with base b and exponent x. The value b is the quantity that the y value is multiplied by each time the x value is increased by 1. When looking at a table of values, an exponential function can be identified because the $f(x)$ values are being multiplied. (In contrast, linear $f(x)$ values are being added to.)

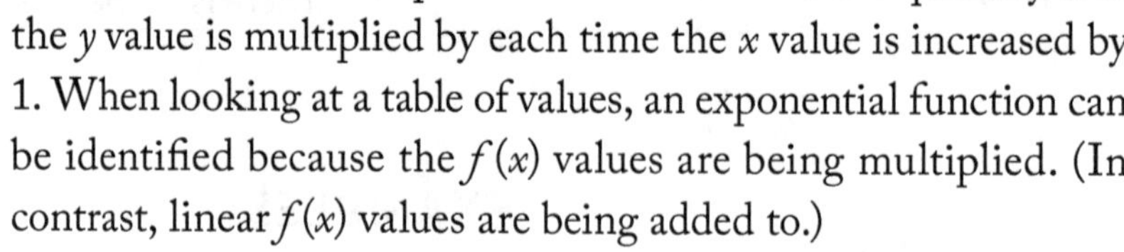

DID YOU KNOW?

To solve an exponential equation, start by looking for a common base:

$4^{(x-2)}=\sqrt{8}$

can be rewritten as

$(2^2)^{(x-2)}=(2^3)^{\frac{1}{2}}$

If no common base can be found, logarithms can be used to move the variable out of the exponent position.

The graph of the exponential parent function does not cross the x-axis, which is the function's horizontal asymptote. The y-intercept of the function is at (0, 1).

The general formula for an exponential function, $f(x) = ab^{(x-h)}+k$, allows for transformations to be made to the function. The value h moves the function left or right (moving the y-intercept) while the value k moves the function up or down (moving both the y-intercept and the horizontal asymptote). The value a stretches or compresses the function (moving the y-intercept).

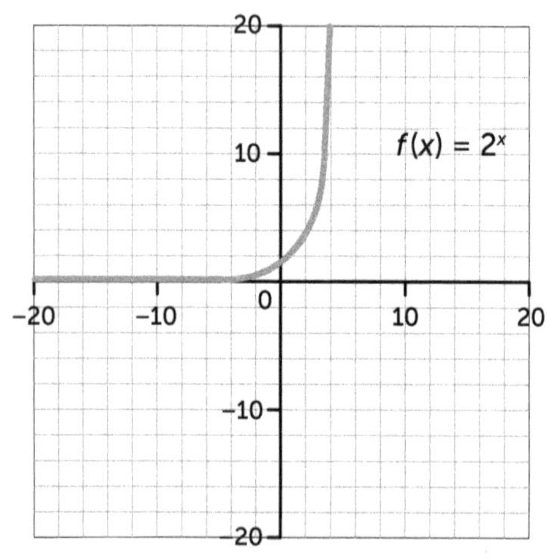

Figure 2.13. Exponential Parent Function

Exponential equations have at least one variable in an exponent position. One way to solve these equations is to make the bases on both side of the equation equivalent, and then equate the exponents. Many exponential equations do not have a solution. Negative numbers often lead to no solutions: for example, $2^x = -8$. The domain of exponential functions is only positive numbers, as seen above, so there is no x value that will result in a negative output.

EXAMPLES

60. Graph the exponential function $f(x) = 5^x - 2$.

61. If the height of grass in a yard in a humid summer week grows by 5% every day, how much taller would the grass be after six days?

62. Solve for x: $4^{x+1} = \frac{1}{256}$

LOGARITHMIC FUNCTIONS

The **LOGARITHMIC FUNCTION (LOG)** is the inverse of the exponential function.

A log is used to find out to what power an input is raised to get a desired output. In the table, the base is 3. The log function determines to what power 3 must be raised so that $\frac{1}{9}$ is the result in the table (the answer is –2). As with all inverse functions, these exponential and logarithmic functions are reflections of each other across the line $y = x$.

$y = \log_3 x \Rightarrow 3^y = x$

x	y
$\frac{1}{9}$	-2
$\frac{1}{3}$	-1
1	0
3	1
9	2
27	3

A **NATURAL LOGARITHM (LN)** has the number e as its base. Like π, e is an irrational number that is a nonterminating decimal. It is usually shortened to 2.71 when doing calculations. Although the proof of e is beyond the scope of this book, e is to be understood as the upper limit of the range of this rational function: $\left(1 + \frac{1}{n}^n\right)$.

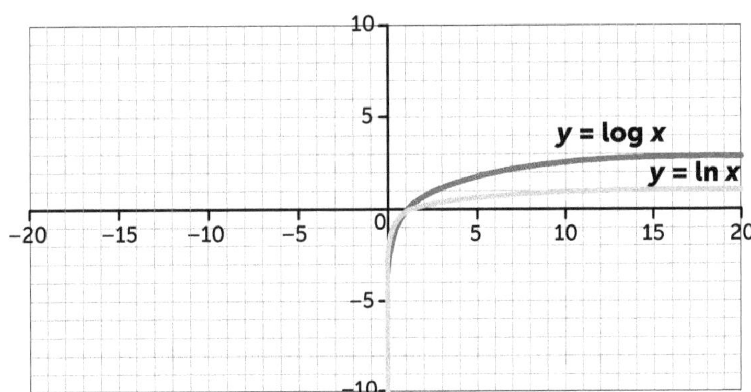

Figure 2.14. Logarithmic Parent Functions

In order to make use of and solve logarithmic functions, log rules are often employed that allow simplification:

Table 2.7. Properties of Logarithms

Change of base	$\log_b(m) = \frac{\log(m)}{\log(b)}$
Logs of products	$\log_b(mn) = \log_b(m) + \log_b(n)$
Logs of quotients	$\log_b\left(\frac{m}{n}\right) = \log_b(m) - \log_b(n)$
Log of a power	$\log_b(m^n) = n \times \log_b(m)$
Equal logs/equal arguments	$\log_b M = \log_b N \Leftrightarrow M = N$

Note that when the base is not written out, such as in $\log(m)$, it is understood that the base is 10. Just like a 1 is not put in front of a variable because its presence is implicitly understood, 10 is the implicit base whenever a base is not written out.

EXAMPLES

63. Expand $\log_5\left(\frac{25}{x}\right)$

64. Solve for x: $\ln x + \ln 4 = 2\ln 4 - \ln 2$

65. Solve for x: $2^x = 40$

SPECIAL EQUATIONS

There are three exponential function formulas that frequently show up in word problems:

THE GROWTH FORMULA: $y = a(1 + r)^t$
Initial amount a increases at a rate of r per time period

THE DECAY FORMULA: $y = a(1 - r)^t$
Initial amount a decreases at a rate of r per time period

In these formulas, a is the initial amount (at time $t = 0$), r is the rate of growth or decay (written as a decimal in the formula), and t is the number of growth or decay cycles that have passed.

A special case of the growth function is known as:

THE COMPOUND-INTEREST FORMULA: $A = P\left(1 + \frac{r}{n}\right)^{nt}$

In this formula, A is the future value of an investment, P is the initial deposit (or principal), r is the interest rate as a percentage, n is the number of times interest is compounded within a time period, or how often interest is applied to the account in a year (once per year, $n = 1$; monthly, $n = 12$; etc.), and t is the number of compounding cycles (usually years).

EXAMPLES

66. In the year 2000, the number of text messages sent in a small town was 120. If the number of text messages grew every year afterward by 124%, how many years would it take for the number of text messages to surpass 36,000?

67. The half-life of a certain isotope is 5.5 years. If there were 20 grams of one such isotope left after 22 years, what was its original weight?

68. If there were a glitch at a bank and a savings account accrued 5% interest five times per week, what would be the amount earned on a $50 deposit after twelve weeks?

Modeling Relationships

Modeling relationships requires use of one of four of the function types examined above with an appropriate equation for a word problem or scenario.

Table 2.8. Function Types

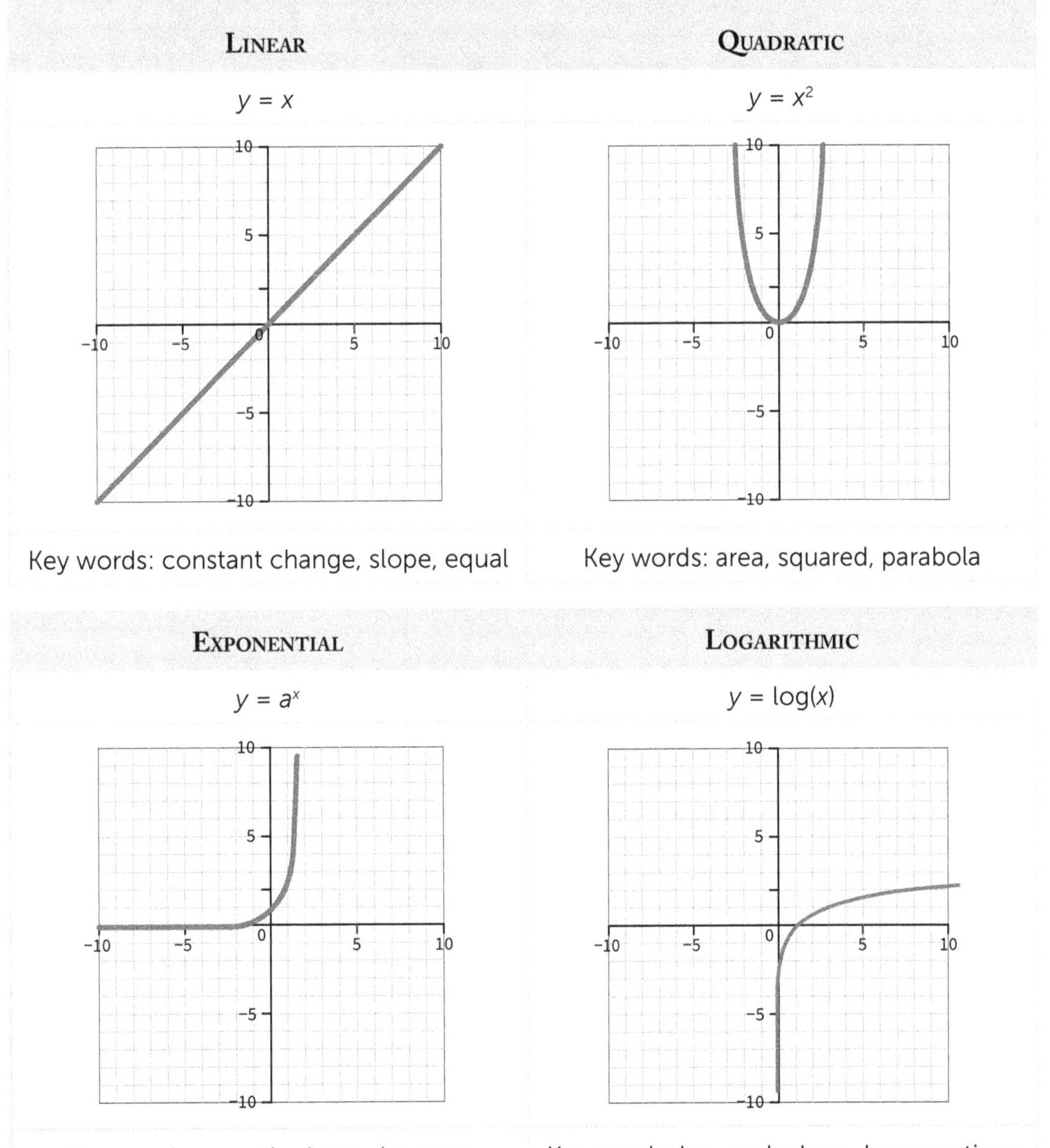

Since exponential functions and log functions are inverses of each other, it will often be the case that exponential or log problems can be solved by either type of equation.

EXAMPLES

69. Consider the following sets of coordinate pairs of a function: {(-1,0.4), (0,1), (2,6.25), and (3,15.625)}. What kind of function does this represent?

70. At a recent sporting event, there were 20,000 people in attendance. When it ended, people left the building at a rate of 1,000 people in the first minute, 1,000 more in the second minute, 1,000 in the third minute, and so on. What equation describes the behavior of attendees leaving the event for every minute after the event finished?

Test Your Knowledge

Work the problem, and then choose the most correct answer.

1. Which of the following is equivalent to $z^3(z + 2)^2 - 4z^3 + 2$?

A) 2

B) $z^5 + 4z^4 + 4z^3 + 2$

C) $z^6 + 4z^3 + 2$

D) $z^5 + 4z^4 + 2$

2. Which of the following represents a linear equation?

A) $\sqrt[3]{y} = x$

B) $\sqrt[3]{x} = y$

C) $\sqrt[3]{y} = x^2$

D) $y = \sqrt[3]{x^3}$

3. Which of the following is the *y*-intercept of the given equation?

$7y - 42x + 7 = 0$

A) $(0, \frac{1}{6})$

B) (6,0)

C) (0,–1)

D) (–1,0)

4. What is the slope of the graph below? Write in the answer:

____

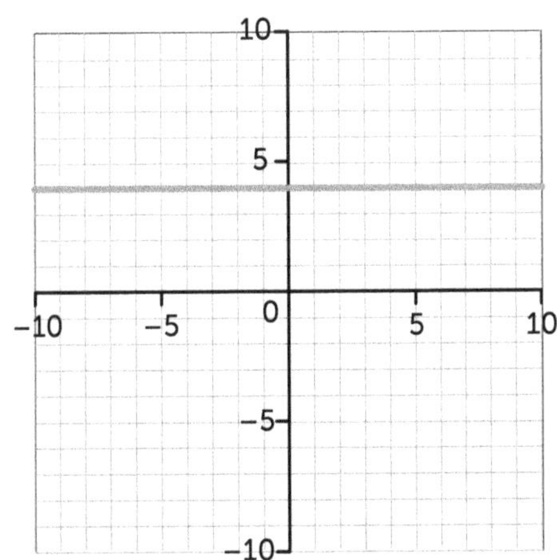

5. 50 shares of a financial stock and 10 shares of an auto stock are valued at $1,300. If 10 shares of the financial stock and 10 shares of the auto stock are valued at $500, what is the value of 50 shares of the auto stock? Write in the answer:

____

6. What are the real zero(s) of the following polynomial?

$2n^2 + 2n - 12 = 0$

A) {2}

B) {–3, 2}

C) {2, 4}

D) There are no real zeros of *n*.

7. What is the solution set for the inequality $2x^2 - 4x - 6 < 0$?

A) (–1, 3)

B) (– •, •)

C) ∅

D) (– •, –1) ∪ (3, •)

8. Which expression is equivalent to $5^2 \times (-5)^{-2} - (2 + 3)^{-1}$?

A) 0

B) 1

C) $\frac{5}{4}$

D) $\frac{4}{5}$

Answer Key

EXAMPLES

1. $5(m-2)^3 + 3m^2 - \frac{m}{4} - 1$

Plug the value 4 in for m in the expression.

$= 5(4-2)^3 + 3(4)^2 - \frac{4}{4} - 1$

Calculate all the expressions inside the parentheses.

$= 5(2)^3 + 3(4)^2 - \frac{4}{4} - 1$

Simplify all exponents.

$= 5(8) + 3(16) - \frac{4}{4} - 1$

Perform multiplication and division from left to right.

$= 40 + 48 - 1 - 1$

Perform addition and subtraction from left to right.

= 86

2. The only like terms in both expressions are $12x$ and $8x$, so these two terms will be added, and all other terms will remain the same.

$a + b = (12x + 8x) + 7xy - 9y - 9xz + 7z =$ $\mathbf{20x + 7xy - 9y - 9xz + 7z}$

3. $5x(x^2 - 2c + 10)$

Distribute and multiply the term outside the parentheses to all three terms inside the parentheses.

$(5x)(x^2) = 5x^3$

$(5x)(-2c) = -10xc$

$(5x)(10) = 50x$

$\mathbf{= 5x^3 - 10xc + 50x}$

4. $(x^2 - 5)(2x - x^3)$

Apply FOIL: first, outside, inside, and last.

$(x^2)(2x) = 2x^3$

$(x^2)(-x^3) = -x^5$

$(-5)(2x) = -10x$

$(-5)(-x^3) = 5x^3$

Combine like terms and put them in order.

$= 2x^3 - x^5 - 10x + 5x^3$

$\mathbf{= -x^5 + 7x^3 - 10x}$

5. $16z^2 + 48z$

Both terms have a z, and 16 is a common factor of both 16 and 48. So the greatest common factor is $16z$. Factor out the GCF.

$16z^2 + 48z$

$\mathbf{= 16z(z + 3)}$

6. $6m^3 + 12m^3n - 9m^2$

All the terms share the factor m^2, and 3 is the greatest common factor of 6, 12, and 9. So, the GCF is $3m^2$.

$\mathbf{= 3m^2(2m + 4mn - 3)}$

7. $16x^2 + 52x + 30$

Remove the GCF of 2.

$= 2(8x^2 + 26x + 15)$

To factor the polynomial in the parentheses, calculate $ac = (8)(15) = 120$, and consider all the pairs of numbers that multiply to be 120: 1×120, 2×60, 3×40, 4×30, 5×24, 6×20, 8×15, and 10×12. Of these pairs, choose the pair that adds to be the b-value 26 (6 and 20).

$= 2(8x^2 + 6x + 20x + 15)$

Group.

$= 2[(8x^2 + 6x) + (20x + 15)]$

Factor out the GCF of each group.

$= 2[(2x(4x + 3) + 5(4x + 3)]$

Factor out the common binomial.

$= 2[(4x + 3)(2x + 5)]$

$\mathbf{= 2(4x + 3)(2x + 5)}$

If there are no values r and s that multiply to be ac and add to be b, then the polynomial is prime and cannot be factored.

8. $-21x^2 - x + 10$

Factor out the negative.

$= -(21x^2 + x - 10)$

Factor the polynomial in the parentheses.

$ac = 210$ and $b = 1$

The numbers 15 and −14 can be multiplied to get 210 and subtracted to get 1.

$= -(21x^2 - 14x + 15x - 10)$

Group.

$= -[(21x^2 - 14x) + (15x - 10)]$

Factor out the GCF of each group.

$= -[7x(3x - 2) + 5(3x - 2)]$

Factor out the common binomial.

$\mathbf{= -(3x - 2)(7x + 5)}$

9. $\frac{100(x + 5)}{20} = 1$

Multiply both sides by 20 to cancel out the denominator.

$(20)\left(\frac{100(x + 5)}{20}\right) = (1)(20)$

$100(x + 5) = 20$

Distribute 100 through the parentheses.

$100x + 500 = 20$

"Undo" the +500 by subtracting 500 on both sides of the equation to isolate the variable term.

$100x = -480$

"Undo" the multiplication by 100 by dividing by 100 on both sides to solve for x.

$x = \frac{-480}{100}$

$\mathbf{x = -4.8}$

10. $2(x + 2)^2 - 2x^2 + 10 = 42$

Eliminate the exponents on the left side.

$2(x + 2)(x + 2) - 2x^2 + 10 = 42$

Apply FOIL.

$2(x^2 + 4x + 4) - 2x^2 + 10 = 42$

Distribute the 2.

$2x^2 + 8x + 8 - 2x^2 + 10 = 42$

Combine like terms on the left-hand side.

$8x + 18 = 42$

Isolate the variable. "Undo" +18 by subtracting 18 on both sides.

$8x = 24$

"Undo" multiplication by 8 by dividing both sides by 8.

$\mathbf{x = 3}$

11. $\frac{A(3B + 2D)}{2N} = 5M - 6$

Multiply both sides by $2N$ to clear the fraction, and distribute the A through the parentheses.

$3AB + 2AD = 10MN - 12N$

Isolate the term with the D in it by moving $3AB$ to the other side of the equation.

$2AD = 10MN - 12N - 3AB$

Divide both sides by $2A$ to get D alone on the right-hand side.

$\mathbf{D = \frac{(10MN - 12N - 3AB)}{2A}}$

12. $6x - 2y - 8 = 0$

Rearrange the equation into slope-intercept form by solving the equation for y.

$-2y = -6x + 8$

$y = \frac{-6x + 8}{-2}$

$y = 3x - 4$

The slope is 3, the value attached to x.

$\boldsymbol{m = 3}$

13. (−2,5) and (−5,3)

Calculate the slope.

$m = \frac{3-5}{(-5)-(-2)} = \frac{-2}{-3} = \frac{2}{3}$

To find b, plug into the equation $y = mx + b$ the slope for m and a set of points for x and y.

$5 = \frac{2}{3}(-2) + b$

$5 = \frac{-4}{3} + b$

$b = \frac{19}{3}$

Replace m and b to find the equation of the line.

$\boldsymbol{y = \frac{2}{3}x + \frac{19}{3}}$

14. The y-intercept can be identified on the graph as (0,3).

$b = 3$

To find the slope, choose any two points and plug the values into the slope equation. The two points chosen here are (2,−1) and (3,−3).

$m = \frac{(-3)-(-1)}{3-2} = \frac{-2}{1} = -2$

Replace m with −2 and b with 3 in $y = mx + b$.

$\boldsymbol{y = -2x + 3}$

15. The line has a rise of 0 and a run of 1, so the slope is $\frac{0}{1} = 0$. There is no x-intercept. The y-intercept is (0,2), meaning that the b-value in the slope-intercept form is 2.

$\boldsymbol{y = 0x + 2}$**, or** $\boldsymbol{y = 2}$

16. Solve the system with substitution. Solve one equation for one variable.

$2x - 4y = 28$

$x = 2y + 14$

Plug in the resulting expression for x in the second equation and simplify.

$4x - 12y = 36$

$4(2y + 14) - 12y = 36$

$8y + 56 - 12y = 36$

$-4y = -20$

$y = 5$

Plug the solved variable into either equation to find the second variable.

$2x - 4y = 28$

$2x - 4(5) = 28$

$2x - 20 = 28$

$2x = 48$

$x = 24$

The answer is $y = 5$ and $x = 24$ or **(24,5)**.

17. Isolate the variable in one equation.

$3 = -4x + y$

$y = 4x + 3$

Plug the expression into the second equation.

Both equations have slope 4. This means the graphs of the equations are parallel lines, so no intersection (solution) exists.

$16x = 4y + 2$

$16x = 4(4x + 3) + 2$

$16x = 16x + 12 + 2$

$0 = 14$

No solution exists.

18. Because solving for x or y in either equation will result in messy fractions, this problem is best solved using elimination. The goal is to eliminate one of the variables by making the coefficients in front of one set of variables the same, but with different signs, and then adding both equations.

To eliminate the x's in this problem, find the least common multiple of coefficients 6 and 4. The smallest number that both 6 and 4 divide into evenly is 12. Multiply the top equation by −2, and the bottom equation by 3.

$6x + 10y = 18 \xrightarrow[(-2)]{} -12x - 20y = -36$

$4x + 15y = 37 \xrightarrow[(3)]{} 12x + 45y = \underline{111}$

Add the two equations to eliminate the x's.

$25y = 75$

Solve for y.

$y = 3$

Replace y with 3 in either of the original equations.

$6x + 10(3) = 18$

$6x + 30 = 18$

$x = -2$

The solution is **(−2,3)**.

19. Write the system in matrix form, $AX = B$.

$$\begin{bmatrix} 2 & -3 \\ 3 & -4 \end{bmatrix} \begin{bmatrix} x \\ y \end{bmatrix} = \begin{bmatrix} -5 \\ -8 \end{bmatrix}$$

Calculate the inverse of Matrix ***A***.

$$\begin{bmatrix} 2 & -3 \\ 3 & -4 \end{bmatrix}^{-1} = \frac{1}{(2)(-4) - (-3)(3)} \begin{bmatrix} -4 & 3 \\ -3 & 2 \end{bmatrix}$$

$$= \begin{bmatrix} -4 & 3 \\ -3 & 2 \end{bmatrix}$$

Multiply ***B*** by the inverse of ***A***.

$$\begin{bmatrix} x \\ y \end{bmatrix} = \begin{bmatrix} -4 & 3 \\ -3 & 2 \end{bmatrix} \begin{bmatrix} -5 \\ -8 \end{bmatrix} = \begin{bmatrix} -4 \\ -1 \end{bmatrix}$$

Match up the 2 × 1 matrices to identify x and y.

$x = -4$

$y = -1$

20. Identify the quantities.

Number of tickets = x

Cost per ticket = 5

Cost for x tickets = $5x$

Total cost = 28

Entry fee = 3

Set up equations. The total cost for x tickets will be equal to the cost for x tickets plus the $3 flat fee.

$5x + 3 = 28$

Solve the equation for x.

$5x + 3 = 28$

$5x = 25$

$x = 5$

The student bought **5 tickets**.

21. Assign variables.

Student price = s

Nonstudent price = n

Create two equations using the number of shirts Kelly sold and the money she earned.

$10s + 4n = 84$

$20s + 10n = 185$

Solve the system of equations using substitution.

$10s + 4n = 84$

$10n = -20s + 185$

$n = -2s + 18.5$

$10s + 4(-2s + 18.5) = 84$

$10s - 8s + 74 = 84$

$2s + 74 = 84$

$2s = 10$

$s = 5$

The student cost for shirts is **$5**.

22. $3z + 10 < -z$

Collect nonvariable terms to one side.

$3z < -z - 10$

Collect variable terms to the other side.

$4z < -10$

Isolate the variable.

$\mathbf{z < -2.5}$

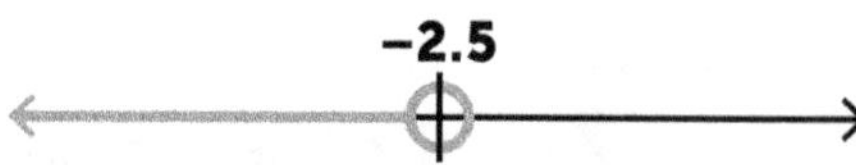

23. $2x - 3 > 5(x - 4) - (x - 4)$

Distribute 5 through the parentheses and −1 through the parentheses.

$2x - 3 > 5x - 20 - x + 4$

Combine like terms.

$2x - 3 > 4x - 16$

Collect x-terms to one side, and constant terms to the other side.

$-2x > -13$

Divide both sides by −2; since dividing by a negative, reverse the direction of the inequality.

$\mathbf{x < 6.5}$

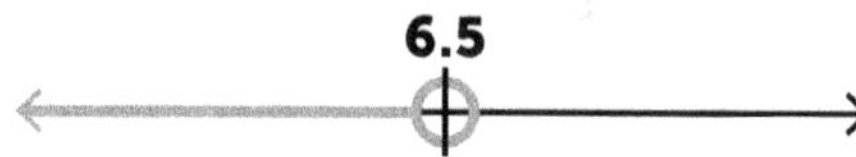

24. $2x + 4 < -18$ *or* $4(x + 2) > 18$

Solve each inequality independently.

$2x < -14$	$4x + 8 > 18$
$x < -7$	$4x > 10$
	$x > 2.5$

The solution to the original compound inequality is **the set of all x for which $x < -7$ or $x > 2.5$**.

25. $-1 \leq 3(x + 2) - 1 \leq x + 3$

Break up the compound inequality into two inequalities.

$-1 \leq 3(x + 2) - 1$ *and*
$3(x + 2) - 1 \leq x + 3$

Solve separately.

$-1 \leq 3x + 6 - 1$	$3x + 6 - 1 \leq x + 3$
$-6 \leq 3x$	$2x \leq -2$
$-2 \leq x$ and	$x \leq -1$

The only values of x that satisfy *both* inequalities are the values between −2 and −1 (inclusive).

$\mathbf{-2 \leq x \leq -1}$

26. Find the x- and y-intercepts.

$3x + 6y \leq 12$

$3(0) + 6y = 12$

$y = 2$

y-intercept: (0,2)

$3x + 6(0) \leq 12$

$x = 4$

x-intercept: (4,0)

Graph the line using the intercepts, and shade below the line.

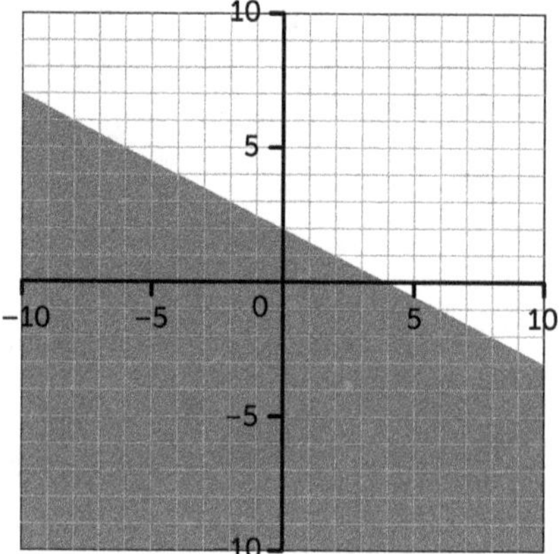

27. To solve the system, graph all three inequalities in the same plane; then identify the area where the three solutions overlap. All

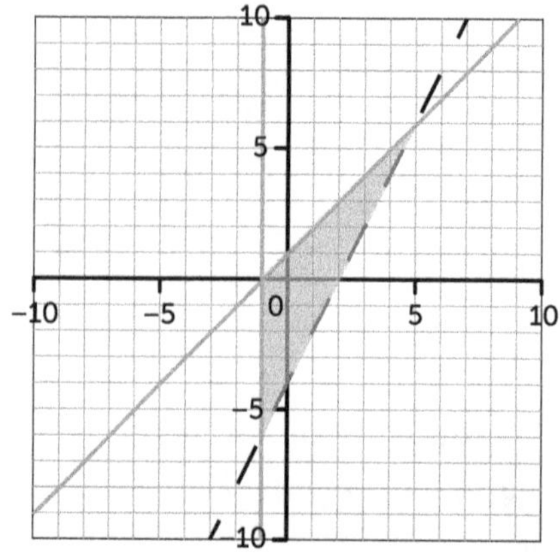

points (x,y) in this area will be solutions to the system since they satisfy all three inequalities.

28. Determine the equation of the boundary line.

y-intercept: (0,2)

slope: 3

$y = 3x + 2$

Replace the equal sign with the appropriate inequality: the line is dotted and the shading is above the line, indicating that the symbol should be "greater than." Check a point: for example (1,5) is a solution since $5 > 3(-1) + 2$.

$\mathbf{y > 3x + 2}$

29. This quadratic is given in vertex form, with $h = -3$ and $k = 2$. The vertex of this equation is (–3,2). The line of symmetry is the vertical line that passes through this point. Since the x-value of the point is –3, the line of symmetry is $\mathbf{x = -3}$.

30. $y = -3x^2 + 24x - 27$

This quadratic equation is in standard form. Use the formula for finding the x-value of the vertex.

$x = -\frac{b}{2a}$ where $a = -3$, $b = 24$

$x = -\frac{24}{2(-3)} = 4$

Plug $x = 4$ into the original equation to find the corresponding y-value.

$y = -3(4)^2 + 24(4) - 27 = 21$

The vertex is at **(4,21)**.

31. $y = -3x^2 + 24x - 27$

Move c to the other side of the equation.

$y + 27 = -3x^2 + 24x$

Divide through by a (–3 in this example).

$\frac{y}{-3} - 9 = x^2 - 8x$

Take half of the new b, square it, and add that quantity to both sides: $\frac{1}{2}(-8) = -4$. Squaring it gives $(-4)2 = 16$.

$\frac{y}{-3} - 9 + 16 = x^2 - 8x + 16$

Simplify the left side, and write the right side as a binomial squared.

$\frac{y}{-3} + 7 = (x - 4)^2$

Subtract 7, and then multiply through by –3 to isolate y.

$\mathbf{y = -3(x - 4)^2 + 21}$

32. Method 1: Make $y = 0$; isolate x by square rooting both sides:

Make $y = 0$.

$0 = -(x + 3)^2 + 1$

Subtract 1 from both sides.

$-1 = -(x + 3)^2$

Divide by –1 on both sides.

$1 = (x + 3)^2$

Square root both sides. Don't forget to write plus OR minus 1.

$(x + 3) = \pm 1$

Write two equations using +1 and –1.

$(x + 3) = 1$ *or* $(x + 3) = -1$

Solve both equations. These are the zeros.

$\mathbf{x = -2}$ **or** $\mathbf{x = -4}$

Method 2: Convert vertex form to standard form, and then use the quadratic formula.

Put the equation in standard form by distributing and combining like terms.

$y = -(x + 3)^2 + 1$

$y = -(x^2 + 6x + 9) + 1$

$y = -x^2 - 6x - 8$

Find the zeros using the quadratic formula.

$$x = \frac{-b \pm \sqrt{(b^2 - 4ac)}}{2a}$$

$$x = \frac{-(-6) \pm \sqrt{(-6)^2 - 4(-1)(-8)}}{2(-1)}$$

$$x = \frac{6 \pm \sqrt{36 - 32}}{-2}$$

$$x = \frac{6 \pm \sqrt{4}}{-2}$$

$\mathbf{x = -4,-2}$

33. This polynomial can be factored in the form $(z - 2)(z - 2) = 0$, so the only root is $z = 2$. There is only one x-intercept, and the vertex of the graph is *on* the x-axis.

34. If the quadratic has zeros at $x = -3$ and $x = 2$, then it has factors of $(x + 3)$ and $(x - 2)$. The quadratic function can be written in the factored form $y = a(x + 3)(x - 2)$. To find the a-value, plug in the point $(-2,8)$ for x and y:

$8 = a(-2 + 3)(-2 - 2)$

$8 = a(-4)$

$a = -2$

The quadratic function is:

$\mathbf{y = -2(x + 3)(x - 2)}$.

35. Start by marking the vertex at $(3,4)$ and recognizing this parabola opens upward. The line of symmetry is $x = 3$. Now, plug in an easy value for x to get one point on the curve; then use symmetry to find another point. In this case, choose $x = 2$ (one unit to the left of the line of symmetry) and solve for y:

$y = 2(2 - 3)^2 + 4$

$y = 2(1) + 4$

$y = 6$

Thus the point $(2,6)$ is on the curve. Then use symmetry to find the corresponding point one unit to the right of the line of symmetry, which must also have a y value of 6. This point is $(4,6)$. Draw a parabola through the points.

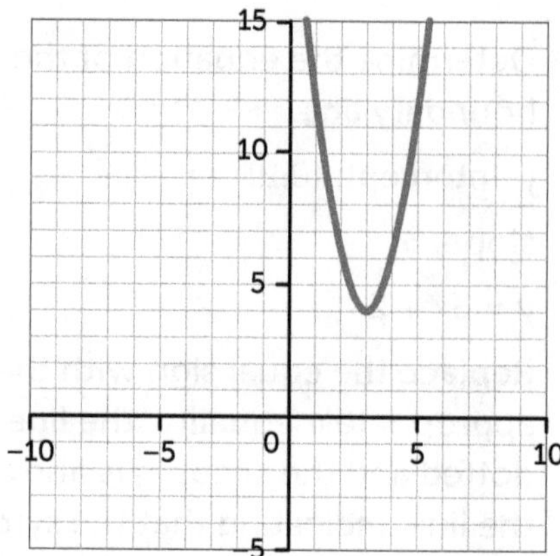

36. Locate the vertex and plug values for h and k into the vertex form of the quadratic equation.

$(h,k) = (0,5)$

$y = a(x - h)^2 + k$

$y = a(x - 0)^2 + 5$

$y = ax^2 + 5$

Choose another point on the graph to plug into this equation to solve for a.

$(x,y) = (1,2)$

$y = ax^2 + 5$

$2 = a(1)^2 + 5$

$a = -3$

Plug a into the vertex form of the equation.

$\mathbf{y = -3x^2 + 5}$

37. Find the zeros of the inequality.

$x^2 - 4x = 12$

$x^2 - 4x - 12 = 0$

$(x + 2)(x - 6) = 0$

$x = -2,6$

Create a table or number line with the intervals created by the zeros. Use a test value to determine whether the expression is positive or negative.

x	$(x + 2)(x - 6)$
$-\infty < x < -2$	+
$-2 < x < 6$	–
$6 < x < \infty$	+

Identify the values of x which make the expression positive.

$\mathbf{x < -2}$ **or** $\mathbf{x > 6}$

38. Set the quantity inside the parentheses equal to 27 or –27, and solve:

$x - 3 = -27$

$x = -24$

$x - 3 = 27$

$\mathbf{x = 30}$

39. The first step is to isolate the absolute value part of the equation. Multiplying both sides by 5 gives:

$|r - 7| = 135$

If the quantity in the absolute value bars is 135 or –135, then the absolute value would be 135:

$r - 7 = -135$

$\mathbf{r = -128}$

$r - 7 = 135$

$\mathbf{r = 142}$

40. $\left|\frac{3x}{7}\right| \geq 4 - x$

Simplify the equation.

$\frac{|3x|}{7} \geq 4 - x$

$|3x| \geq 28 - 7x$

Create and solve two inequalities. When including the negative answer, flip the inequality.

$3x \geq 28 - 7x$

$10x \geq 28$

$x \geq \frac{28}{10}$

$-(3x) \leq 28 - 7x$

$-3x \leq 28 - 7x$

$4x \leq 28$

$x \leq 7$

Combine the two answers to find the solution set.

$\mathbf{\frac{28}{10} \leq x \leq 7}$

41. $f(4)$ if $f(x) = x^3 - 2x + \sqrt{x}$

Plug in 4.

$f(4) = (4)^3 - 2(4) + \sqrt{(4)}$

Follow the PEMDAS order of operations.

$= 64 - 8 + 2 =$ **58**

42. This function has an asymptote at $x = 9$, so is not defined there. Otherwise, the function is defined for all other values of x.

D: $-\infty < x < 9$ *or* $9 < x < \infty$

Interval notation can also be used to show domain and range. Round brackets indicate that an end value is not included, and square brackets show that it is. The symbol ∪ means *or*, and the symbol ∩ means *and*. For example, the statement (–infinity,4) ∪ (4,infinity) describes the set of all real numbers except 4.

Since the function has a horizontal asymptote at $y = 1$ that it never crosses, the function never takes the value 1, so the range is all real numbers except 1:

R: $-\infty < y < 1$ *or* $1 < y < \infty$.

43. For the domain, this graph goes on to the right to positive infinity. Its leftmost point, however, is $x =$ –2. Therefore, its domain is all real numbers equal to or greater than –2, **D:** $\mathbf{-2 \leq x < \infty}$, or $\mathbf{[-2,\infty)}$.

The lowest range value is $y = 2$. Although it has a decreasing slope, this function continues to rise. Therefore, the domain is all real numbers greater than 2, **R: 2 ≤ y < ∞ or [2,∞)**.

44. For a set of numbers to represent a function, every input must generate a unique output. Therefore, if the same input (x) appears more than once in the table, determine if that input has two different outputs. If so, then the table does not represent a function.

A) This table is not a function because input value 1 has two different outputs (1 and 3).

B) Table B is not function because 0 is the only input and results in four different values.

C) This table shows a function because each input has one output.

D) This table also has one input going to two different values, so it is not a function.

45. Replace $f(x)$ with y.

$y = 5x + 5$

Switch the places of y and x.

$x = 5y + 5$

Solve for y.

$x = 5y + 5$

$x - 5 = 5y$

$y = \frac{x}{5} - 1$

$\mathbf{f^{-1}(x) = \frac{x}{5} - 1}$

46. This is a linear graph with some clear coordinates: (–5,0), (0,–1), (5,–2), and (10,–3). This means the inverse function will have coordinate (0,–5), (–1,0), (–2,5), and (–3,10). The inverse function is reflected over the line $y = x$ and is the line $f^{-1}(x) = -5(x + 1)$ below.

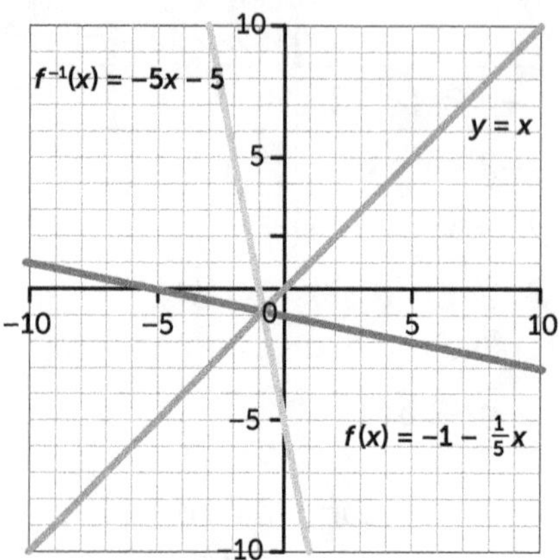

47. $(y \circ z)(-4) = y(z(-4))$

Starting on the inside, evaluate z.

$z(-4)$

$= 3(-4) - 3 = -12 - 3 = -15$

Replace $z(-4)$ with –15, and simplify.

$y(z(-4))$

$= y(-15) = 2(-15) - 1$

$= -30 - 1 = \mathbf{-31}$

48. Replace x in the $k(x)$ function with $\left(\frac{1}{2}x - 2\right)$

$(k \circ t)(x) = k(t(x))$

$= k\left(\frac{1}{2}x - 2\right) = \frac{1}{2}\left(\frac{1}{2}x - 2\right) - 3$

Simplify.

$= \frac{1}{4}x - 1 - 3 = \frac{1}{4}x - 4$

$\mathbf{(k\ 0\ t)(x) = \frac{1}{4x} - 4}$

49. $N(4) = 400(4) = 1600$ and means that 4 hours after the park opens there are 1600 people in the park. $W(N(4)) = W(1600) = 96$ and means that 4 hours after the park opens the wait time is about **96 minutes** for the ride.

50. This function is the absolute value function with a vertical shift up of 4 units (since the 4 is outside the absolute value bars), and a horizontal shift left of 1 unit (since it is inside the bars). The vertex of the graph is at (–1,4) and the line $x = -1$ is an axis of symmetry.

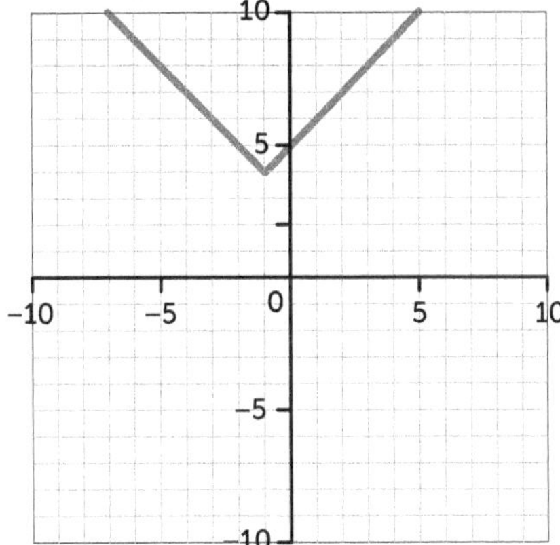

51. The negative sign in front of the absolute value means the graph will be reflected across the x-axis, so it will open down. The 3 causes a vertical stretch of the function, which results in a narrower graph. The basic curve is shifted 2 units right (since the –2 is an inside change) and 2 units up (since the +2 is an outside change), so the vertex is at (2,2).

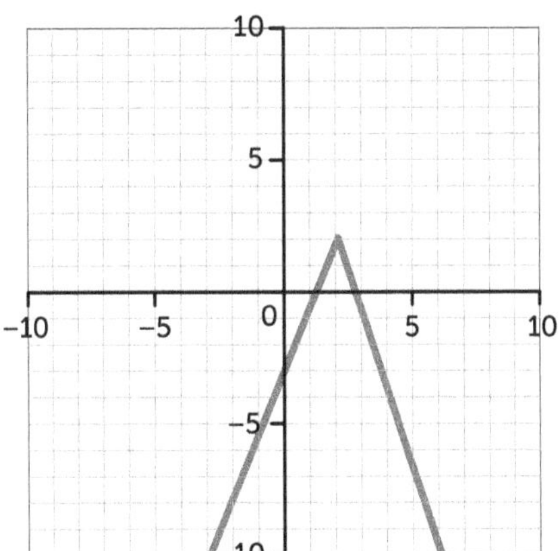

52. $y = 3t^4 - 48$

Factor the polynomial. Remove the common factor of 3 from each term and make $y = 0$.

$3(t^4 - 16) = 0$

Factor the difference of squares.

$t^2 - 4$ is also a difference of squares.

$3(t^2 - 4)(t^2 + 4) = 0$

$3(t + 2)(t - 2)(t^2 + 2) = 0$

Set each factor equal to zero. Solve each equation.

$t + 2 = 0$	$t - 2 = 0$	$t^2 + 2 = 0$
$t = -2$	$t = 2$	$t^2 = -2$
$t = \pm\sqrt{-2} = \pm 2i$		

This degree 4 polynomial has four roots, two real roots: **2 or –2**, and two complex roots: **$2i$ or $-2i$**. The graph will have two x-intercepts at (–2,0) and (2,0).

53. Write the difference.

$f(x) - g(x) = \frac{2}{3x^2y} - \frac{5}{21y}$

Figure out the least common denominator. Every factor must be represented to the highest power it appears in either denominator. So, the LCD = $3(7)x^2y$.

$= \frac{2}{3x^2y}\left(\frac{7}{7}\right) - \frac{5}{21y}\left(\frac{x^2}{x^2}\right)$

$= \frac{14}{21x^2y} - \frac{5x^2}{21x^2y}$

Subtract the numerators the find the answer.

$f(x) - g(x) = \mathbf{\frac{14 - 5x^2}{21x^2y}}$

54. Write the quotient; then invert and multiply.

$\frac{f(x)}{g(x)} = \frac{\frac{(x-1)(x+2)^2}{5x^2+10x}}{\frac{x^2+x-2}{x+5}}$

$= \frac{(x-1)(x+2)^2}{5x^2+10x} \times \frac{x+5}{x^2+x-2}$

Factor all expressions, and then cancel any factors that appear in both the numerator and the denominator.

$= \frac{(x-1)(x+2)^2}{5x(x+2)} \times \frac{x+5}{(x+2)(x-1)}$

$= \mathbf{\frac{x+5}{5x}}$

55. $\frac{x}{x+2} + \frac{2}{x^2+5x+6} = \frac{5}{x+3}$

Factor any denominators that need factoring.

$$\frac{x}{x+2} + \frac{2}{(x+3)(x+2)} = \frac{5}{x+3}$$

Multiply through by the LCM of the denominators, which is $(x + 2)(x + 3)$.

$x(x + 3) + 2 = 5(x + 2)$

Simplify the expression.

$x^2 + 3x + 2 - 5x - 10 = 0$

$x^2 - 2x - 8 = 0$

Factor the quadratic.

$(x - 4)(x + 2) = 0$

Plugging $x = -2$ into the original equation results in a 0 in the denominator. So this solution is an extraneous solution and must be thrown out.

Plugging in $x = 4$ gives:

$\frac{4}{6} + \frac{2}{16 + 20 + 6} = \frac{5}{7}$.

So $\mathbf{x = 4}$ is a solution to the equation.

56. The numerator will have a factor of $(x - 5)$ in order to have a zero at $x = 5$. The denominator will need factors of $(x - 1)$ and $(x + 1)$ in order for the denominator to be 0 when x is 1 or -1. Thus, one function that would have these features is

$$y = \frac{(x-5)}{(x+1)(x-1)} = \mathbf{\frac{x-5}{x^2-1}}$$

57. $f(x) = \frac{3x^2 - 12x}{x^2 - 2x - 3}$.

Factor the equation.

$$y = \frac{3x^2 - 12x}{x^2 - 2x - 3} \quad \frac{3x(x-4)}{(x-3)(x+1)}$$

Find the roots by setting the numerator equal to zero.

$3x(x - 4) = 0$

$x = 0,4$

Find the vertical asymptotes by setting the denominator equal to zero.

$(x - 3)(x + 1) = 0$

$x = -1,3$

Find the horizontal asymptote by looking at the degree of the numerator and the denominator.

The degree of the numerator and denominator are equal, so the asymptote is the ratio of the coefficients:

$y = \frac{3}{1} = 3$

Use the roots and asymptotes to graph the function.

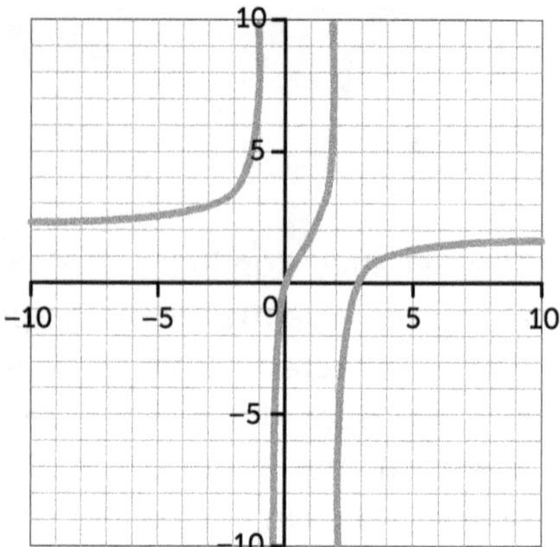

58. $\sqrt{2x - 5} + 4 = x$

Isolate the $\sqrt{2x - 5}$ by subtracting 4.

$\sqrt{2x - 5} = x - 4$

Square both sides to clear the $\sqrt{}$.

$2x - 5 = x^2 - 8x + 16$

Collect all variables to one side.

$x^2 - 10x + 21 = 0$

Factor and solve.

$(x - 7)(x - 3) = 0$

$x = 7$ or $x = 3$

Check solutions by plugging into the original, as squaring both sides can cause extraneous solutions.

True, $x = 7$ is a solution.

False, $x = 3$ is NOT a solution (extraneous solution).

$\sqrt{2(7) - 5} + 4 = 7$

$\sqrt{2(3) - 5} + 4 = 3$

$\sqrt{9} + 4 = 7$

$\sqrt{1} + 4 = 3$

$\mathbf{x = 7}$

59. $2(x^2 - 7x)^{\frac{2}{3}} = 8$

Divide by 2 to isolate the radical.

$(x^2 - 7x)^{\frac{2}{3}} = 4$

Raise both sides to the $\frac{3}{2}$ power to clear the $\frac{2}{3}$ exponent.

$x^2 - 7x = 4^{\frac{3}{2}}$

$x^2 - 7x = 8$

This is a quadratic, so collect all terms to one side.

$x^2 - 7x - 8 = 0$

Factor and solve for x.

$(x - 8)(x + 1) = 0$

$\mathbf{x = 8}$ or $\mathbf{x = -1}$

Plugging both solutions into the original equation confirms that both are solutions.

60. One way to do this is to use a table:

x	$5^x - 2$
–2	$\frac{1}{25} - 2 = -\frac{49}{25}$
–1	$\frac{1}{5} - 2 = -\frac{9}{5}$
0	$1 - 2 = -1$
1	$5 - 2 = 3$
2	$25 - 2 = 23$

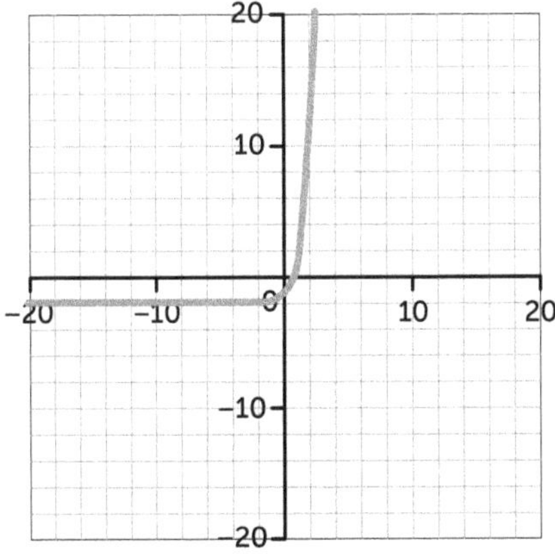

Another way to graph this is simply to see this function as the parent function $y = b^x$ (with $b = 5$), shifted down by a vertical shift of 2 units. Thus the new horizontal asymptote will be at $y = 2$, and the new y-intercept will be $y = -1$.

61. Any time a question concerns growth or decay, an exponential function must be created to solve it. In this case, create a table with initial value a, and a daily growth rate of (1+0.05) = 1.05 per day.

Days (x)	Height (h)
0	a
1	$1.05a$
2	$1.05(1.05a) = (1.05)^2a$
3	$(1.05)^2(1.05a) = (1.05)^3a$
x	$(1.05)^xa$

After six days the height of the grass is $(1.05)^6$ = **1.34 times as tall.** The grass would grow 34% in one week.

62. $4^{x+1} = \frac{1}{256}$

Find a common base and rewrite the equation.

$4^{x+1} = 4^{-4}$

Set the exponents equal and solve for x.

$x + 1 = -4$

$\mathbf{x = -5}$

63. Since division of a term can be written as a subtraction problem, this simplifies to:

$\log_5(25) - \log_5(x)$

The first term asks "what power of 5 gives 25?" The power is 2. Therefore, the most expanded form is: $\mathbf{2 - \log_5(x)}$

64. $\ln x + \ln 4 = 2\ln 4 - \ln 2$

Apply the log of product and log of exponent rules.

$\ln(4x) = \ln 4^2 - \ln 2$

$\ln(4x) = \ln 16 - \ln 2$

Follow log of quotient rule.

$\ln(4x) = \ln 8$

Set the arguments equal to each other.

$4x = 8$

$\mathbf{x = 2}$

65. $2^X = 40$

Take the $\log_2$ of both sides.

$\log_2 2^X = \log_2 40$

Drop the *x* down using properties of logs.

$x\log_2 2 = \log_2 40$

$\text{Log}_2 2$ simplifies to 1.

$x = \log_2 40$

Use the change of base rule or a calculator to calculate the value of $\log_2(40)$.

$\approx$ **5.32**

66. Plug the given values into the growth equation.

$y = a(1 + r)^t$

$36{,}000 = 120(1 + 1.24)^t$

Use the properties of logarithms to solve the equation.

$300 = (2.24)^t$

$\log_{2.24} 300 = \log_{2.24}(2.24)^t$

$7.07 \approx t$

The number of text messages will pass 36,000 in **7.07 years**.

67. Identify the variables.

$t = \frac{22}{5.5} = 4$

$r = 0.5$

$a = ?$

Plug these values into the decay formula and solve.

$20 = a(1 - 0.50)^4$

$20 = a(0.5)^4$

$20 = a\left(\frac{1}{2}\right)^4$

$20 = a\left(\frac{1}{16}\right)$

$320 = a$

The original weight is **320 grams**.

68. Identify the variables.

$r = 0.05$

$n = 5$

$t = 12$

$P = 50$

Use the compound-interest formula, since this problem has many steps of growth within a time period.

$A = 50\left(1 + \frac{0.05}{5}\right)^{5(12)}$

$A = 50(1.01)^{60}$

$A = 50(1.82) = 90.83$

Subtract the original deposit to find the amount of interest earned.

$90.83 - 50 =$ **$40.83**

69. Graphing on the coordiante plane shows what looks like an exponential function.

If it is exponential, then its equation is $y = ab^x$, where *a* is the *y*-intercept, so $a = 1$ in this case. The *b* is the growth or decay value. Plug in another point, such as (2, 6.25) to solve for *b*:

$y = ab^x$

$6.25 = (1)b^2$

$b = \sqrt{6.25} = 2.5$

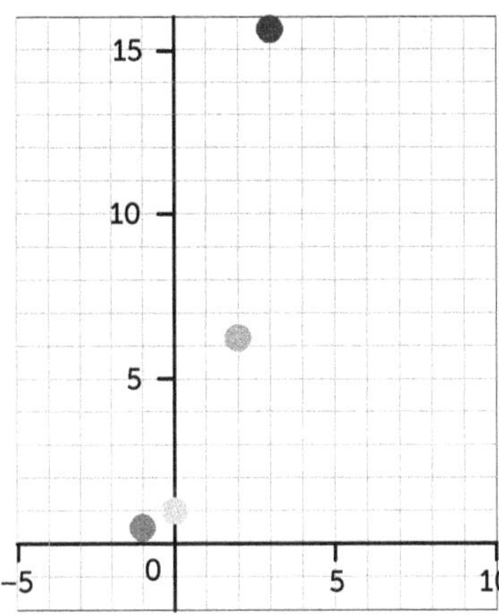

The equation, then, is $y = 2.5^x$.

Check another point to confirm: Is $0.4 = 2.5^{-1}$? Since $2.5 = \frac{5}{2}$, and $\left(\frac{5}{2}\right)^{-1} = \frac{2}{5} = 0.4$, the equation works. The function is **exponential**.

70. The dependent variable is the number of attendees leaving the event (y). There is a constant change of 1,000 people per minute. Note that this is an additive pattern in the table: every increase of 1 in time results in a subtraction of the same value (1,000) in y. Because it is a constant rate of change, a linear model is required:

$y = 20{,}000 - 1{,}000x$

Here 20,000 is the y-intercept, and the rate of change, –1,000, is the slope.

To test this model, confirm that 18,000 attendees were left in the building after two minutes:

$y = 20{,}000 - 1{,}000(2) = 18{,}000$

The model is correct.

TEST YOUR KNOWLEDGE

1. **D) is correct.** Simplify using PEMDAS.

   $z^3(z + 2)^2 - 4z^3 + 2$

   $z^3(z^2 + 4z + 4) - 4z^3 + 2$

   $z^5 + 4z^4 + 4z^3 - 4z^3 + 2$

   $\mathbf{z^5 + 4z^4 + 2}$

2. **D) is correct.** Solve each equation for y and find the equation with a power of 1.

   $\sqrt[3]{y} = x \rightarrow y = x^3$

   $\sqrt[3]{x} = y \rightarrow y = \sqrt[3]{x}$

   $\sqrt[3]{y} = x^2 \rightarrow y = x^6$

   $y = \sqrt[3]{x^3} \rightarrow \mathbf{y = x}$

3. **C) is correct.** Plug 0 in for x and solve for y.

   $7y - 42x + 7 = 0$

   $7y - 42(0) + 7 = 0$

   $y = -1$

   The y-intercept is at **(0,−1)**.

4. The slope of a horizontal line is always 0.

5. Set up a system of equations and solve using elimination.

   f = the cost of a financial stock

   a = the cost of an auto stock

   $50f + 10a = 1300$

   $10f + 10a = 500$

   $50f + 10a = 1300$

   $\underline{+ -50f - 50a = -2500}$

   $-40a = -1{,}200$

   $a = 30$

   $50(30) = \mathbf{1{,}500}$

6. **B) is correct.** Factor the trinomial and set each factor equal to 0.

   $2n^2 + 2n - 12 = 0$

   $2(n^2 + n - 6) = 0$

   $2(n + 3)(n - 2) = 0$

   $\mathbf{n = -3}$ and $\mathbf{n = 2}$

7. **A) is correct.** Use the zeros of the function to find the intervals where it is less than 0.

   $2x^2 - 4x - 6 = 0$

   $(2x - 6)(x + 1) = 0$

   $x = 3$ and $x = -1$

   $(-\bullet,-1) \rightarrow 2x^2 - 4x - 6 > 0$

   $(-1,3) \rightarrow 2x^2 - 4x - 6 < 0$

   $(3,\bullet) \rightarrow 2x^2 - 4x - 6 > 0$

   The function is less than 0 on the interval **(−1,3)**.

8. **D) is correct.** Simplify using PEMDAS.

   $5^2 \times (-5)^{-2} - 5^{-1}$

   $= 25 \times \frac{1}{25} - \frac{1}{5}$

   $= 1 - \frac{1}{5} = \mathbf{\frac{4}{5}}$

CHAPTER THREE
Geometry

Properties of Shapes

BASIC DEFINITIONS

The basic figures from which many other geometric shapes are built are points, lines, and planes. A **POINT** is a location in a plane. It has no size or shape, but is represented by a dot. It is labeled using a capital letter.

A **LINE** is a one-dimensional collection of points that extends infinitely in both directions. At least two points are needed to define a line, and any points that lie on the same line are **COLINEAR**. Lines are represented by two points, such as A and B, and the line symbol: ($\overleftrightarrow{AB}$). Two lines on the same plane will intersect unless they are **PARALLEL**, meaning they have the same slope. Lines that intersect at a 90 degree angle are **PERPENDICULAR**.

A **LINE SEGMENT** has two endpoints and a finite length. The length of a segment, called the measure of the segment, is the distance from A to B. A line segment is a subset of a line, and is also denoted with two points, but with a segment symbol: ($\overline{AB}$). The **MIDPOINT** of a line segment is the point at which the segment is divided into two equal parts. A line, segment, or plane that passes through the midpoint of a segment is called a **BISECTOR** of the segment, since it cuts the segment into two equal segments.

A **RAY** has one endpoint and extends indefinitely in one direction. It is defined by its endpoint, followed by any other point on the ray: $\overrightarrow{AB}$. It is important that the first letter represents the endpoint. A ray is sometimes called a half line.

A **PLANE** is a flat sheet that extends indefinitely in two directions (like an infinite sheet of paper). A plane is a two-dimensional (2D) figure. A plane can always be defined through any three noncollinear points in three-dimensional (3D) space. A plane is named using any three points that are in the plane (for example, plane ABC). Any points lying in the same plane are said to be **COPLANAR**. When two planes intersect, the intersection is a line.

Table 3.1. Basic Geometric Figures

TERM	DIMENSIONS	GRAPHIC	SYMBOL
point	zero	●	$\cdot A$
line segment	one	A •———• B	$\overline{AB}$
ray	one	A •———→ B	$\overrightarrow{AB}$
line	one	←———→	$\overleftrightarrow{AB}$
plane	two	▱	Plane M

EXAMPLE

1. Which points and lines are not contained in plane M in the diagram below?

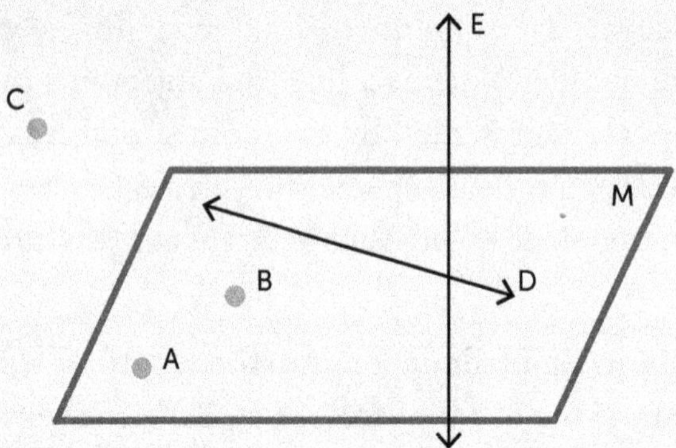

ANGLES

ANGLES are formed when two rays share a common endpoint. They are named using three letters, with the vertex point in the middle (for example $\angle ABC$, where B is the vertex). They can also be labeled with a number or named by their vertex alone (if it is clear to do so). Angles are also classified based on their angle measure. A **RIGHT ANGLE** has a measure of exactly 90°. **ACUTE ANGLES** have measures that are less than 90°, and **OBTUSE ANGLES** have measures that are greater than 90°.

DID YOU KNOW?
Angles can be measured in degrees or radian. Use the conversion factor 1 rad = 57.3 degrees to convert between them.

Any two angles that add to make 90° are called **COMPLEMENTARY ANGLES**. A 30° angle would be complementary to a 60° angle.

SUPPLEMENTARY ANGLES add up to 180°. A supplementary angle to a 60° angle would be a 120° angle; likewise, 60° is the **SUPPLEMENT** of 120°. The complement and supplement of any angle must always be positive. For example, a 140 degree has no complement. Angles that are next to each other and share a common ray are called **ADJACENT ANGLES.** Angles that are adjacent and supplementary are called a **LINEAR PAIR** of angles. Their nonshared rays form a line (thus the *linear* pair). Note that angles that are supplementary do not need to be adjacent; their measures simply need to add to 180°.

VERTICAL ANGLES are formed when two lines intersect. Four angles will be formed; the vertex of each angle is at the intersection point of the lines. The vertical angles across from each other will be equal in measure. The angles adjacent to each other will be linear pairs and therefore supplementary.

A ray, line, or segment that divides an angle into two equal angles is called an **ANGLE BISECTOR.**

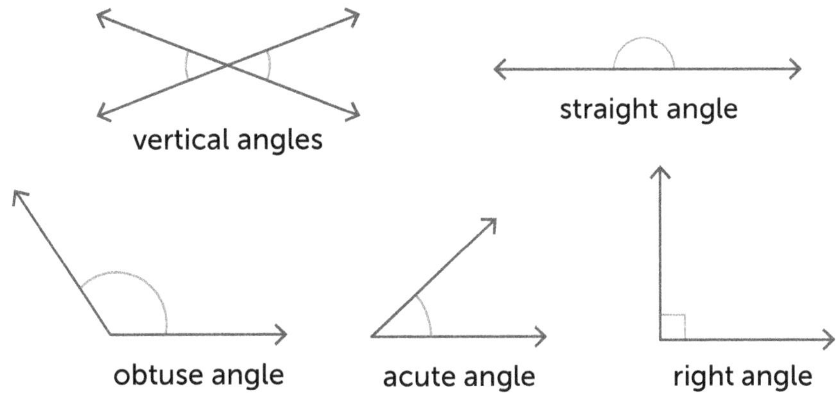

Figure 3.1. Types of Angles

EXAMPLES

2. How many linear pairs of angles are there in the following figure?

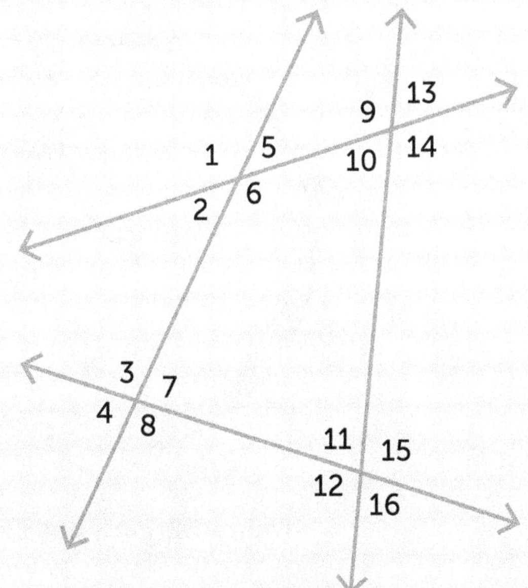

> **3.** If angles *M* and *N* are supplementary and $\angle M$ is 30° less than twice $\angle N$, what is the degree measurement of each angle?

CIRCLES

A **CIRCLE** is the set of all the points in a plane that are the same distance from a fixed point called the **CENTER.** The distance from the center to any point on the circle is the **RADIUS** of the circle. The distance around the circle (the perimeter) is called the **CIRCUMFERENCE.**

DID YOU KNOW?

Trying to square a circle means attempting to create a square that has the same area as a circle. Because the area of a circle depends on ϖ, which is an irrational number, this task is impossible. The phrase is often used to describe trying to do something that can't be done.

The ratio of a circle's circumference to its diameter is a constant value called pi (π), an irrational number which is commonly rounded to 3.14. The formula to find a circle's circumference is $C = 2\pi r$. The formula to find the enclosed area of a circle is $A = \pi r^2$.

Circles have a number of unique parts and properties:

- The **DIAMETER** is the largest measurement across a circle. It passes through the circle's center, extending from one side of the circle to the other. The measure of the diameter is twice the measure of the radius.
- A line that cuts across a circle and touches it twice is called a **SECANT** line. The part of a secant line that lies within a circle is called a **CHORD.** Two chords within a circle are of equal length if they are are the same distance from the center.
- A line that touches a circle or any curve at one point is **TANGENT** to the circle or the curve. These lines are always exterior to the circle. A line tangent to a circle and a radius drawn to the point of tangency meet at a right angle (90°).
- An **ARC** is any portion of a circle between two points on the circle. The **MEASURE** of an arc is in degrees, whereas the **LENGTH OF THE ARC** will be in linear measurement (such as centimeters or inches). A **MINOR ARC** is the small arc between the two points (it measures less than 180°), whereas a **MAJOR ARC** is the large arc between the two points (it measures greater than 180°).
- An angle with its vertex at the center of a circle is called a **CENTRAL ANGLE.** For a central angle, the measure of the arc intercepted by the sides of the angle (in degrees) is the same as the measure of the angle.

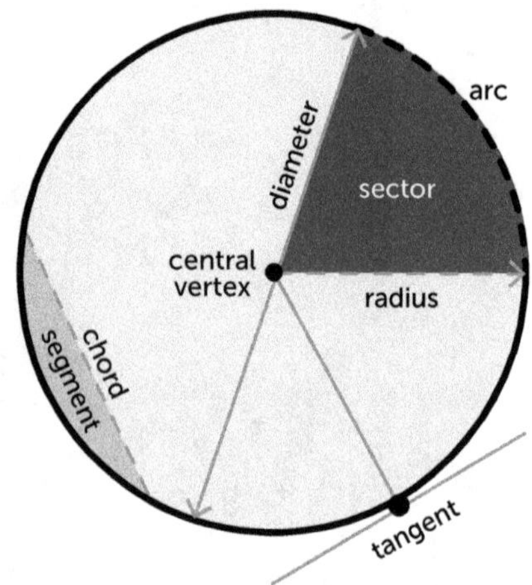

Figure 3.2. Parts of a Circle

- A **SECTOR** is the part of a circle *and* its interior that is inside the rays of a central angle (its shape is like a slice of pie).

	Area of Sector	Length of an Arc
Degrees	$A = \frac{\theta}{360^\circ} \times \pi r^2$	$s = \frac{\theta}{360^\circ} \times 2\pi r$
Radians	$A = \frac{1}{2}\pi^2\theta$	$s = r\theta$

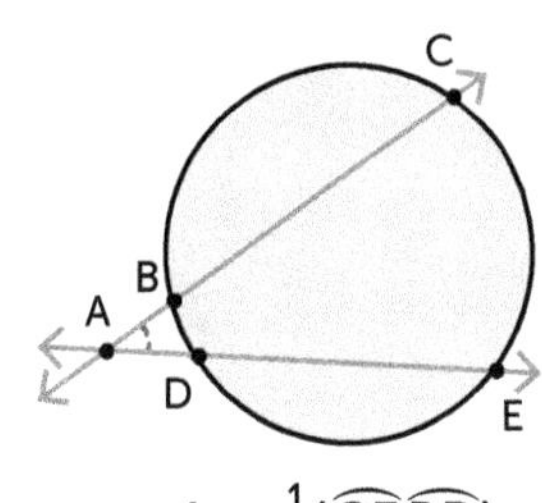

$m\angle A = \frac{1}{2}(\widehat{CE}\widehat{BD})$

Figure 3.3. Angles Outside a Circle

- An **INSCRIBED ANGLE** has a vertex on the circle and is formed by two chords that share that vertex point. The angle measure of an inscribed angle is one-half the angle measure of the central angle with the same endpoints on the circle.
- A **CIRCUMSCRIBED ANGLE** has rays tangent to the circle. The angle lies outside of the circle.
- Any angle outside the circle, whether formed by two tangent lines, two secant lines, or a tangent line and a secant line, is equal to half the difference of the intercepted arcs.
- Angles are formed within a circle when two chords intersect in the circle. The measure of the smaller angle formed is half the sum of the two smaller arc measures (in degrees). Likewise, the larger angle is half the sum of the two larger arc measures.

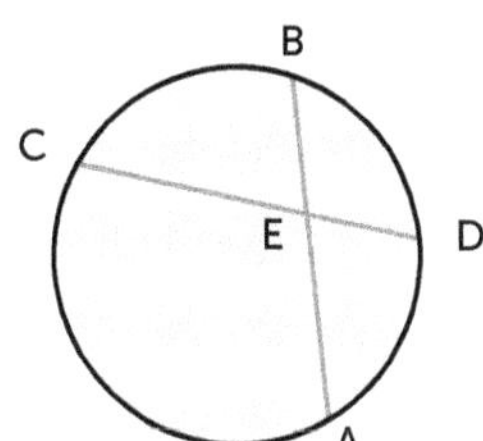

$m\angle E = \frac{1}{2}(\widehat{AC} + \widehat{BD})$

Figure 3.4. Intersecting Chords

- If a chord intersects a line tangent to the circle, the angle formed by this intersection measures one half the measurement of the intercepted arc (in degrees).

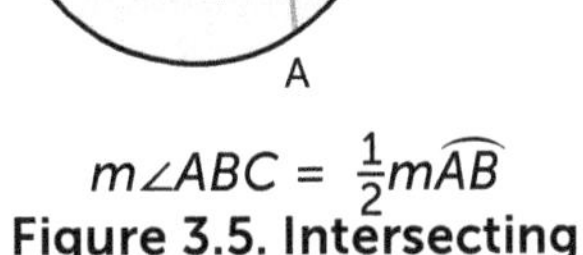

$m\angle ABC = \frac{1}{2}m\widehat{AB}$

Figure 3.5. Intersecting Chord and Tangent

EXAMPLES

4. Find the area of the sector *NHS* of the circle below with center at *H*:

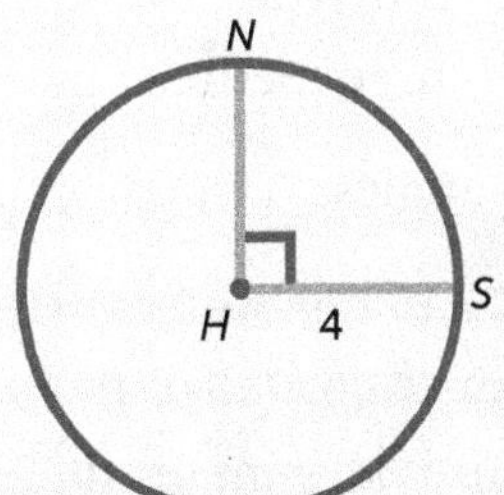

5. In the circle below with center *O*, the minor arc *ACB* measures 5 feet. What is the measurement of $m\angle AOB$?

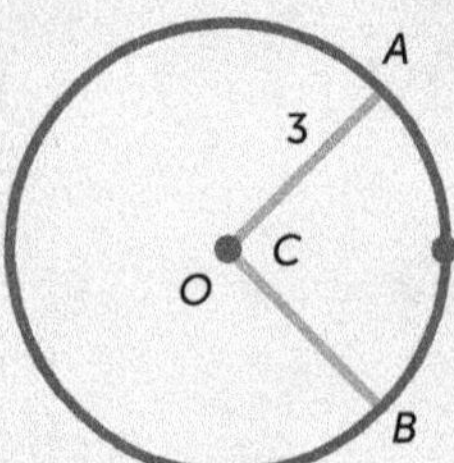

TRIANGLES

Much of geometry is concerned with triangles as they are commonly used shapes. A good understanding of triangles allows decomposition of other shapes (specifically polygons) into triangles for study.

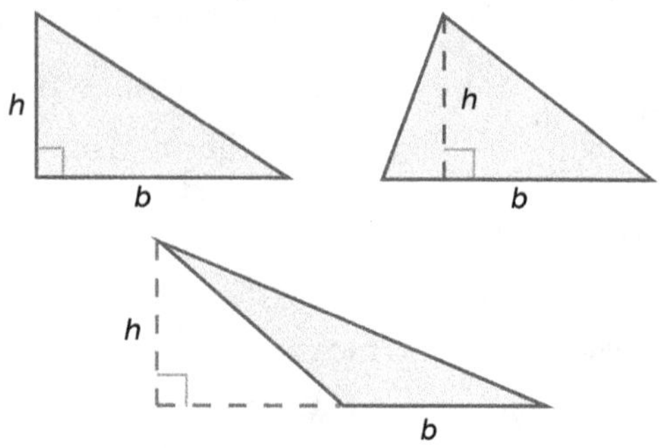

Figure 3.6. Finding the Base and Height of Triangles

Triangles have three sides, and the three interior angles always sum to 180°. The formula for the area of a triangle is $A = \frac{1}{2}bh$ or one-half the product of the base and height (or altitude) of the triangle.

Some important segments in a triangle include the angle bisector, the altitude, and the median. The **ANGLE BISECTOR** extends from the side opposite an angle to bisect that angle. The **ALTITUDE** is the shortest distance from a vertex of the triangle to the line containing the base side opposite that vertex. It is perpendicular to that line and can occur on the outside of the triangle. The **MEDIAN** extends from an angle to bisect the opposite side.

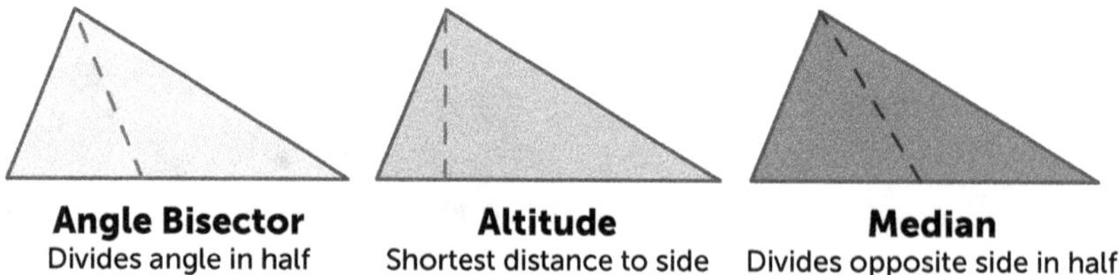

Figure 3.7. Critical Segments in a Triangle

Triangles have two "centers." The **ORTHOCENTER** is formed by the intersection of a triangle's three altitudes. The **CENTROID** is where a triangle's three medians meet.

Triangles can be classified in two ways: by sides and by angles.

A **SCALENE TRIANGLE** has no equal sides or angles. An **ISOSCELES TRIANGLE** has two equal sides and two equal angles, often called **BASE ANGLES**. In an **EQUILATERAL TRIANGLE**, all three sides are equal as are all three angles. Moreover, because the sum of the angles of a triangle is always 180°, each angle of an equilateral triangle must be 60°.

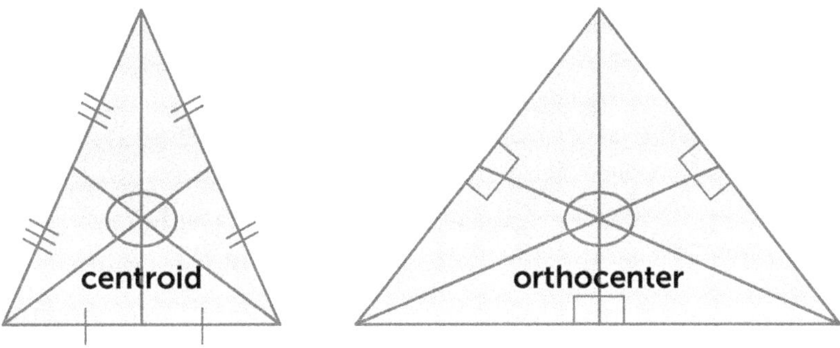

Figure 3.8. Centroid and Orthocenter of a Triangle

A **RIGHT TRIANGLE** has one right angle (90°) and two acute angles. An **ACUTE TRIANGLE** has three acute angles (all angles are less than 90°). An **OBTUSE TRIANGLE** has one obtuse angle (more than 90°) and two acute angles.

Triangles Based on Sides

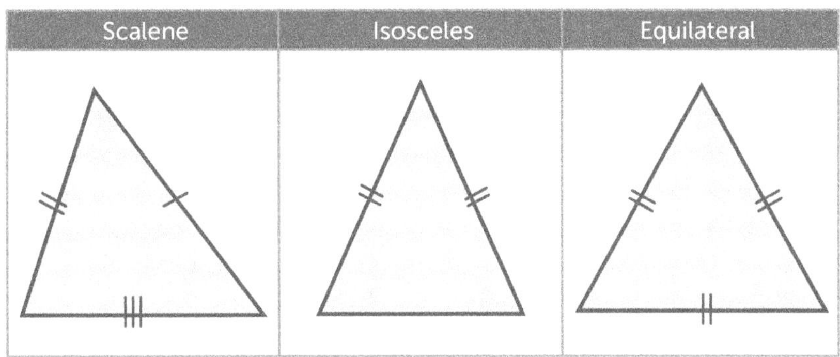

Triangles Based on Angles

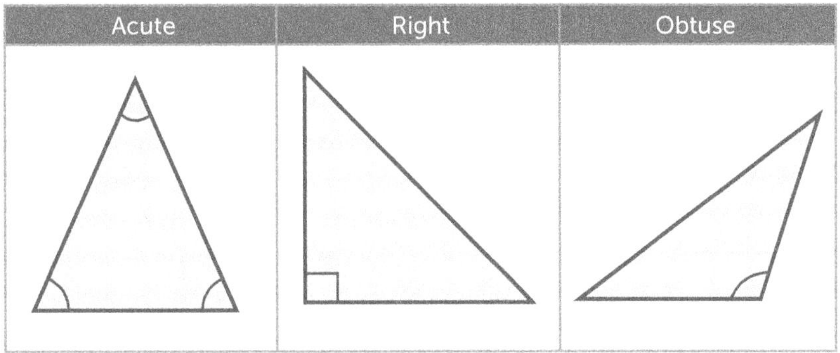

Figure 3.9. Types of Triangles

For any triangle, the side opposite the largest angle will have the longest length, while the side opposite the smallest angle will have the shortest length. The **TRIANGLE INEQUALITY THEOREM** states that the sum of any two sides of a triangle must be greater than the third side. If this inequality does not hold, then a triangle cannot be formed. A consequence of this theorem is the **THIRD-SIDE RULE**: if b and c are two sides of a triangle, then the measure of the third side a must be between

DID YOU KNOW?

Trigonometric functions can be employed to find missing sides and angles of a triangle.

the sum of the other two sides and the difference of the other two sides: $c - b < a < c + b$.

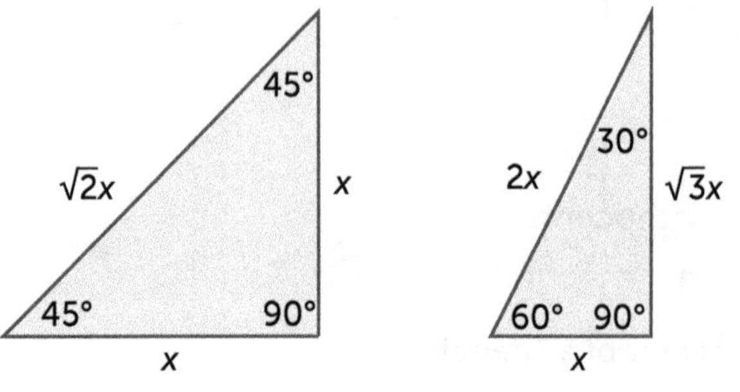

Figure 3.10. Special Right Triangles

Solving for missing angles or sides of a triangle is a common type of triangle problem. Often a right triangle will come up on its own or within another triangle. The relationship among a right triangle's sides is known as the **PYTHAGOREAN THEOREM:** $a^2 + b^2 = c^2$, where c is the hypotenuse and is across from the 90° angle. Right triangles with angle measurements of 90° – 45° – 45° and 90° – 60° – 30° are known as "special" right triangles and have specific relationships between their sides and angles.

EXAMPLES

6. What are the minimum and maximum values of x to the nearest hundredth?

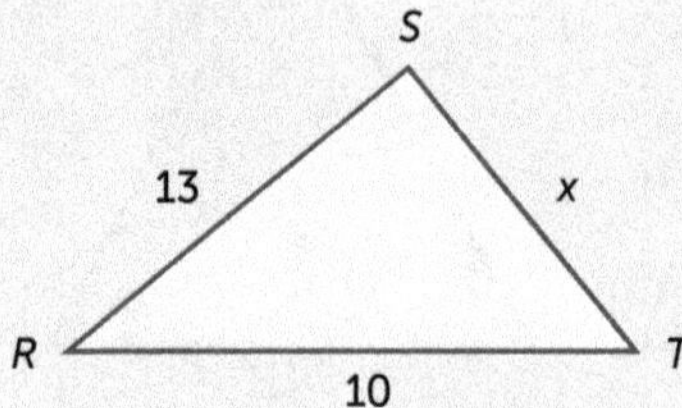

7. Given the diagram, if $XZ = 100$, $WZ = 80$, and $XU = 70$, then $WY = ?$

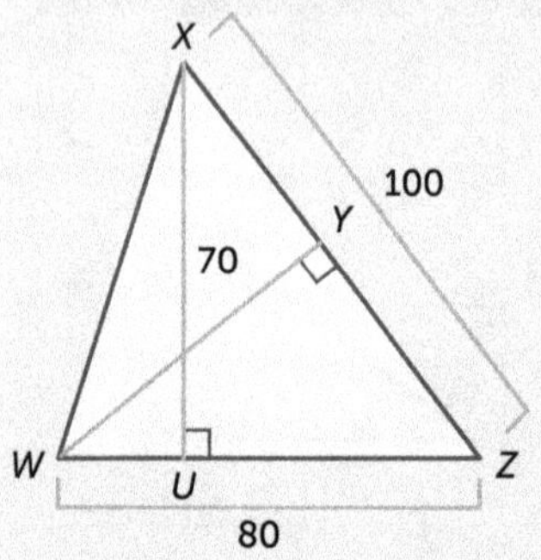

8. Examine and classify each of the following triangles:

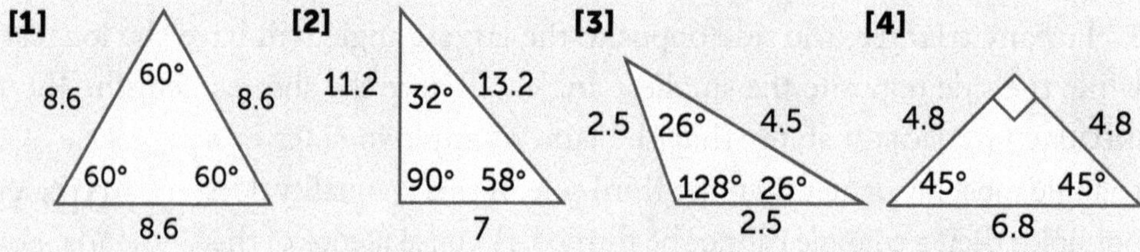

QUADRILATERALS

All closed, four-sided shapes are **QUADRILATERALS**. The sum of all internal angles in a quadrilateral is always 360°. (Think of drawing a diagonal to create two triangles. Since each triangle contains 180°, two triangles, and therefore the quadrilateral, must contain 360°.) The **AREA OF ANY QUADRILATERAL** is $A = bh$, where b is the base and h is the height (or altitude).

A **PARALLELOGRAM** is a quadrilateral with two pairs of parallel sides. A rectangle is a parallelogram with two pairs of equal sides and four right angles. A **KITE** also has two pairs of equal sides, but its equal sides are consecutive. Both a **SQUARE** and a **RHOMBUS** have four equal sides. A square has four right angles, while a rhombus has a pair of acute opposite angles and a pair of obtuse opposite angles. A **TRAPEZOID** has exactly one pair of parallel sides.

DID YOU KNOW?

All squares are rectangles and all rectangles are parallelograms; however, not all parallelograms are rectangles and not all rectangles are squares.

Table 3.2 Properties of Parallelograms

Term	Shape	Properties
Parallelogram		Opposite sides are parallel. Consecutive angles are supplementary. Opposite angles are equal. Opposite sides are equal. Diagonals bisect each other.
Rectangle		All parallelogram properties hold. Diagonals are congruent *and* bisect each other. All angles are right angles.
Square		All rectangle properties hold. All four sides are equal. Diagonals bisect angles. Diagonals intersect at right angles and bisect each other.
Kite		One pair of opposite angles is equal. Two pairs of consecutive sides are equal. Diagonals meet at right angles.
Rhombus		All four sides are equal. Diagonals bisect angles. Diagonals intersect at right angles and bisect each other.
Trapezoid		One pair of sides is parallel. Bases have different lengths. Isosceles trapezoids have a pair of equal sides (and base angles).

EXAMPLES

9. In parallelogram *ABCD*, the measure of angle *m* is is $m° = 260°$. What is the measure of $n°$?

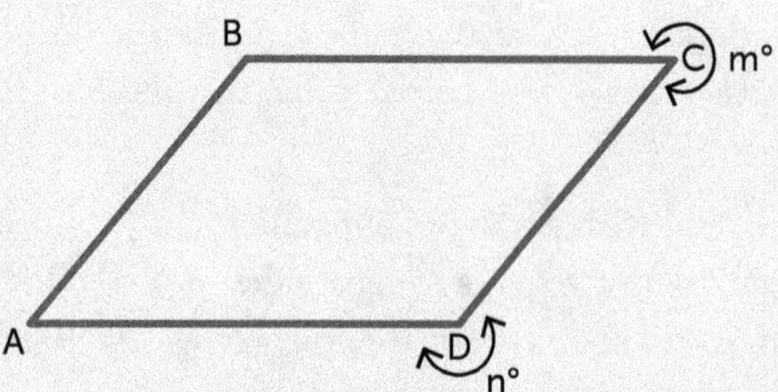

10. A rectangular section of a football field has dimensions of *x* and *y* and an area of 1000 square feet. Three additional lines drawn vertically divide the section into four smaller rectangular areas as seen in the diagram below. If all the lines shown need to be painted, calculate the total number of linear feet, in terms of *x*, to be painted.

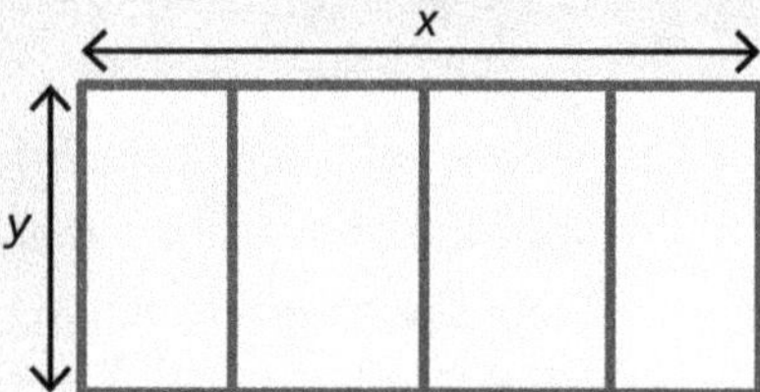

POLYGONS

Any closed shape made up of three or more line segments is a polygon. In addition to triangles and quadrilaterals, **HEXAGONS** and **OCTAGONS** are two common polygons.

DID YOU KNOW?
Breaking an irregular polygon down into triangles and quadrilaterals helps in finding its area.

The two polygons depicted in Figure 3.11 are **REGULAR POLYGONS**, meaning that they are equilateral (all sides having equal lengths) and equiangular (all angles having equal measurements). Angles inside a polygon are **INTERIOR ANGLES**, whereas those formed by one side of the polygon and a line extending outside the polygon are **EXTERIOR ANGLES**:

The sum of the all the exterior angles of a polygon is always 360°. Dividing 360° by the number of a polygon's sides finds the measure of the polygon's exterior angles.

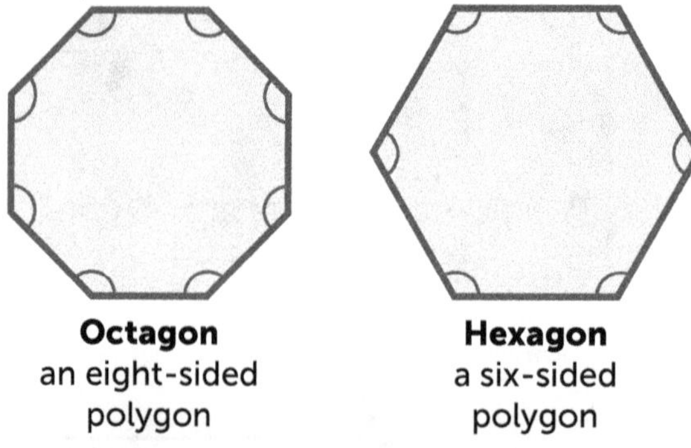

Octagon
an eight-sided polygon

Hexagon
a six-sided polygon

Figure 3.11. Common Polygons

To determine the sum of a polygon's interior angles, choose one vertex and draw diagonals from that vertex to each of the other vertices, decomposing the polygon into multiple triangles. For example, an octagon has six triangles within it, and therefore the sum of the interior angles is $6 \times 180°$ $= 1080°$. In general, the formula for finding the sum of the angles in a polygon is *sum of angles* $= (n - 2) \times 180°$, where n is the number of sides of the polygon.

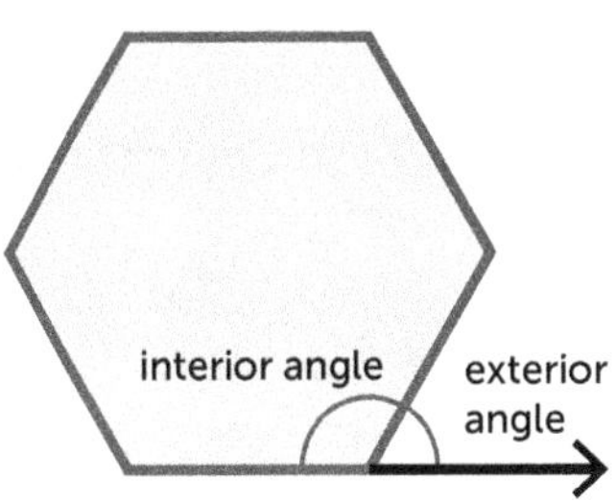

Figure 3.12. Interior and Exterior Angles

To find the measure of a single interior angle in a regular polygon, simply divide the sum of the interior angles by the number of angles (which is the same as the number of sides). So, in the octagon example, each angle is $\frac{1080}{8} = 135°$.

In general, the formula to find the measure of a regular polygon's interior angles is: $\textit{interior angle} = \frac{(n-2)}{n} \times 180°$ where n is the number of sides of the polygon.

To find the area of a polygon, it is helpful to know the perimeter of the polygon (p), and the **APOTHEM** (a). The apothem is the shortest (perpendicular) distance from the polygon's center to one of the sides of the polygon. The formula for the area is: $\textit{area} = \frac{ap}{2}$.

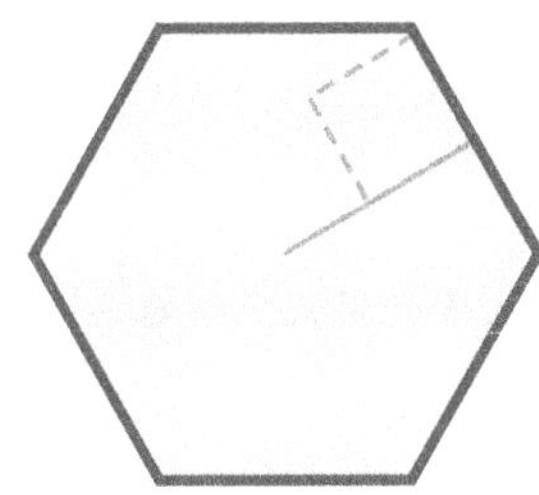

Figure 3.13. Apothem in a Hexagon

Finally, there is no universal way to find the perimeter of a polygon (when the side length is not given). Often, breaking the polygon down into triangles and adding the base of each triangle all the way around the polygon is the easiest way to calculate the perimeter.

EXAMPLES

11. What is the measure of an exterior angle and an interior angle of a regular 400-gon?

12. The circle and hexagon below both share center point *T*. The hexagon is entirely inscribed in the circle. The circle's radius is 5. What is the area of the shaded area?

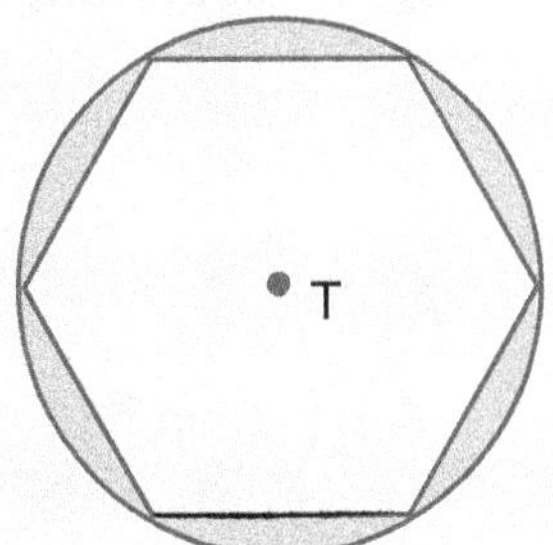

Three-Dimensional Shapes

THREE-DIMENSIONAL SHAPES have depth in addition to width and length. **VOLUME** is expressed as the number of cubic units any solid can hold—that is, what it takes to fill it up. **SURFACE AREA** is the sum of the areas of the two-dimensional figures that are found on its surface. Some three-dimensional shapes also have a unique property called a slant height (ℓ), which is the distance from the base to the apex along a lateral face.

Finding the surface area of a three-dimensional solid can be made easier by using a **NET.** This two-dimensional "flattened" version of a three-dimensional shape shows the component parts that comprise the surface of the solid.

Table 3.3. Three-Dimensional Shapes and Formulas

TERM	SHAPE	FORMULA	
Prism		$V = Bh$ $SA = 2lw + 2wh + 2lh$ $d^2 = a^2 + b^2 + c^2$	B = area of base h = height l = length w = width d = longest diagonal
Cube		$V = s^3$ $SA = 6s^2$	s = cube edge
Sphere		$V = \frac{4}{3}\pi r^3$ $SA = 4\pi r^2$	r = radius
Cylinder		$V = Bh = \pi r^2 h$ $SA = 2\pi r^2 + 2\pi rh$	B = area of base h = height r = radius
Cone		$V = \frac{1}{3}\pi r^2 h$ $SA = \pi r^2 + \pi rl$	r = radius h = height l = slant height
Pyramid		$V = \frac{1}{3}Bh$ $SA = B + \frac{1}{2}(p)l$	B = area of base h = height p = perimeter l = slant height

EXAMPLES

13. A sphere has a radius z. If that radius is increased by t, by how much is the surface area increased? Write the answer in terms of z and t.

14. A cube with volume 27 cubic meters is inscribed within a sphere such that all of the cube's vertices touch the sphere. What is the length of the sphere's radius?

Test Your Knowledge

Work the problem, and then choose the most correct answer.

1. Line *a* and line *b* are perpendicular and intersect at the point (–100,100). If (–95,115) is a point on line *b*, which of the following could be a point on line *a*?

   A) (104,168)

   B) (–95,115)

   C) (–112,104)

   D) (–112,–104)

2. Which of the angles in the figure below are congruent?

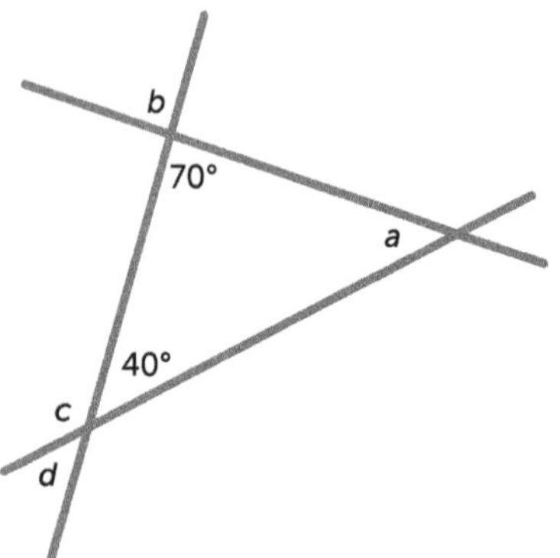

   A) *a* and *d*

   B) *b* and *d*

   C) *a* and *b*

   D) *c* and *b*

3. If angles *a* and *b* are congruent, what is the measurement of angle *c*? Write in the answer:

   ____

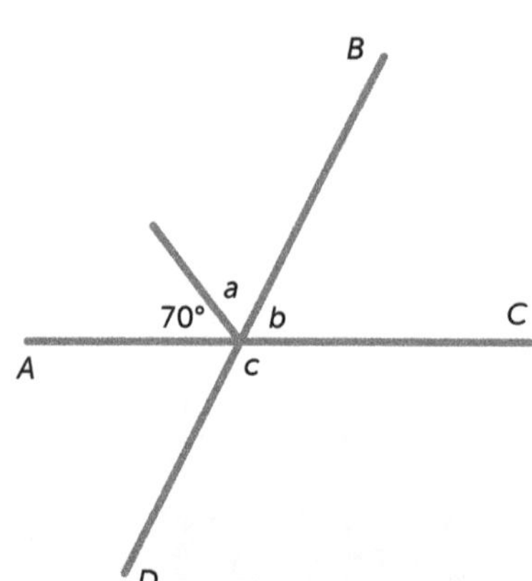

4. A cube is inscribed in a sphere such that each vertex on the cube touches the sphere. If the volume of the sphere is 972π cm^3, what is the approximate volume of the cube in cubic centimeters?

   A) 9

   B) 10.4

   C) 1125

   D) 1729

5. In the *xy*-coordinate plane, how many points have a distance of four from the origin?

   A) 0

   B) 2

   C) 4

   D) •

6. Which of the following sets of shapes are NOT all similar to each other?

   A) right triangles

   B) spheres

   C) 30–60–90 triangles

   D) squares

7. Cone *A* is similar to cone *B* with a scale factor of 3:4. If the volume of cone *A* is 54π, what is the volume of cone *B*? Write in the answer:

   ____

8. If the surface area of a cylinder with radius of 4 feet is 48π square feet, what is its volume? Write in the answer:

   ____

Answer Key

EXAMPLES

1. Points *A* and *B* and line *D* are all on plane *M*. Point *C* is above the plane, and line *E* cuts through the plane and thus does not lie on plane *M*. The point at which line *E* intersects plane *M* is on plane *M* but the line as a whole is not.

2. Any two adjacent angles that are supplementary are linear pairs, so there are 16 linear pairs in the figure ($\angle 1$ and $\angle 5$, $\angle 2$ and $\angle 6$, $\angle 5$ and $\angle 6$, $\angle 2$ and $\angle 1$, and so on).

3. Set up a system of equations.

   $\angle M + \angle N = 180°$

   $\angle M = 2\angle N - 30°$

   Use substitution to solve for $\angle N$.

   $\angle M + \angle N = 180°$

   $(2\angle N - 30°) + \angle N = 180°$

   $3\angle N - 30° = 180°$

   $3\angle N = 210°$

   $\angle N =$ **70°**

   Solve for $\angle M$ using the original equation.

   $\angle M + \angle N = 180°$

   $\angle M + 70° = 180°$

   $\angle M =$ **110°**

4. Identify the important parts of the circle.

   $r = 4$

   $\angle NHS = 90°$

   Plug these values into the formula for the area of a sector.

   $A = \frac{\theta}{360°} \times \pi r^2$

   $= \frac{90}{360} \times \pi(4)^2 = \frac{1}{4} \times 16\pi$

   $=$ **4π**

5. Identify the important parts of the circle.

   $r = 3$

   length of $\overline{ACB} = 5$

   Plug these values into the formula for the length of an arc and solve for θ.

   $s = \frac{\theta}{360°} \times 2\pi r$

   $5 = \frac{\theta}{360°} \times 2\pi(3)$

   $\frac{5}{6\pi} = \frac{\theta}{360°}$

   $\theta = 95.5°$

   $m\angle AOB = 95.5°$

6. The sum of two sides is 23 and their difference is 3. To connect the two other sides and enclose a space, *x* must be less than the sum and greater than the difference (that is, $3 < x < 23$). Therefore, ***x*'s minimum value to the nearest hundredth is 3.01 and its maximum value is 22.99.**

7. $WZ = b_1 = 80$

   $XU = h_1 = 70$

   $XZ = b_2 = 100$

   $WY = h_2 = ?$

   The given values can be used to write two equation for the area of $\triangle WXZ$ with two sets of bases and heights.

   $A = \frac{1}{2}bh$

   $A_1 = \frac{1}{2}(80)(70) = 2800$

   $A_2 = \frac{1}{2}(100)(h_2)$

   Set the two equations equal to each other and solve for *WY*.

   $2800 = \frac{1}{2}(100)(h_2)$

$h_2 = 56$

$\mathbf{WY = 56}$

8. **Triangle 1 is an equilateral triangle** (all 3 sides are equal, and all 3 angles are equal)

   Triangle 2 is a scalene, right triangle (all 3 sides are different, and there is a 90° angle)

   Triangle 3 is an obtuse, isosceles triangle (there are 2 equal sides and, consequently, 2 equal angles)

   Triangle 4 is a right, isosceles triangle (there are 2 equal sides and a 90° angle)

9. Find $\angle C$ using the fact that the sum of $\angle C$ and m is 360°.

   $260° + m\angle C = 360°$

   $m\angle C = 100°$

   Solve for $\angle D$ using the fact that consecutive interior angles in a quadrilateral are supplementary.

   $m\angle C + m\angle D = 180°$

   $100° + m\angle D = 180°$

   $m\angle D = 80°$

   Solve for n by subtracting $m\angle D$ from 360°.

   $m\angle D + n = 360°$

   $\mathbf{n = 280°}$

10. Find equations for the area of the field and length of the lines to be painted (L) in terms of x and y.

    $A = 1000 = xy$

    $L = 2x + 5y$

    Substitute to find L in terms of x.

    $y = \frac{1000}{x}$

    $L = 2x + 5y$

    $L = 2x + 5\left(\frac{1000}{x}\right)$

    $\mathbf{L = 2x + \frac{5000}{x}}$

11. The sum of the exterior angles is 360°. Dividing this sum by 400 gives $\frac{360°}{400}$ = **0.9°**. Since an interior angle is supplementary to an exterior angle, all the interior angles have measure 180 – 0.9 = **179.1°**. Alternately, using the formula for calculating the interior angle gives the same result:

    $\textit{interior angle} = \frac{400-2}{400} \times 180°$

    $= 179.1°$

12. The area of the shaded region will be the area of the circle minus the area of the hexagon. Use the radius to find the area of the circle.

    $A_C = \pi r^2 = \pi(5)^2 = 25\pi$

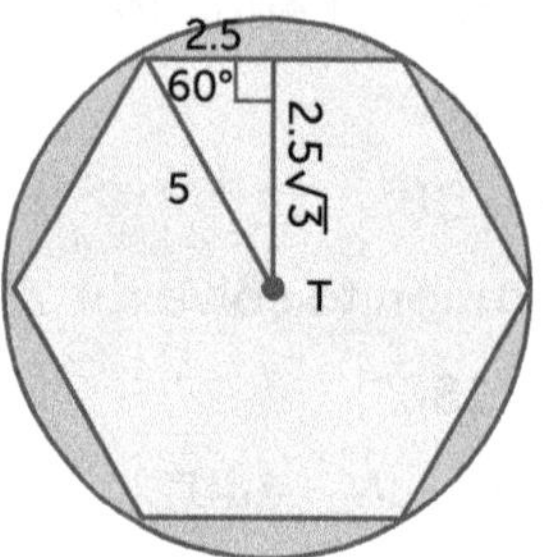

    To find the area of the hexagon, draw a right triangle from the vertex, and use special right triangles to find the hexagon's apothem. Then, use the apothem to calculate the area.

    $a = 2.5\sqrt{3}$

    $A_H = \frac{ap}{2} = \frac{(2.5\sqrt{3})(30)}{2} = 64.95$

    Subtract the area of the hexagon from the circle to find the area of the shaded region.

    $= A_C - A_H$

    $= 25\pi - 2.5\sqrt{3}$

    $\mathbf{\approx 13.59}$

13. Write the equation for the area of the original sphere.

    $SA_1 = 4\pi z^2$

Write the equation for the area of the new sphere.

$SA_2 = 4\pi(z + t)^2$

$= 4\pi(z^2 + 2zt + t^2)$

$= 4\pi z^2 + 8\pi zt + 4\pi t^2$

To find the difference between the two, subtract the original from the increased surface area:

$A_2 - A_1 = 4\pi z^2 + 8\pi zt + 4\pi t^2 - 4\pi z^2$

$= 4\pi t^2 + 8\pi zt$

14. Since the cube's volume is 27, each side length is equal to $\sqrt[3]{27}$ = 3. The long diagonal distance from one of the cube's vertices to its opposite vertex will provide the sphere's diameter:

$d = \sqrt{3^2 + 3^2 + 3^2} = \sqrt{27} = 5.2$

Half of this length is the radius, which is **2.6 meters**.

TEST YOUR KNOWLEDGE

1. **C) is correct.** Find the slope of line *b*, take the negative reciprocal to find the slope of *a*, and test each point.

$(x_1, y_1) = (-100,100)$

$(x_2, y_2) = (-95,115)$

$m_b = \frac{115 - 100}{-95 - (-100)} = \frac{15}{5} = 3$

$m_a = -\frac{1}{3}$

$(104,168)$: $\frac{100 - 168}{-100 - (104)} = \frac{1}{3}$

$(-95,115)$: $\frac{100 - 115}{-100 - (-95)} = 3$

$(-112,104)$: $\frac{100 - 104}{-100 - (-112)} = -\frac{1}{3}$

$(-112,-104)$: $\frac{100 - (-104)}{-100 - (-112)} = 17$

2. **C) is correct.** Find the measure of each angle.

$m\angle a = 180 - (70 + 40) = 70°$

$m\angle b = 70°$

$m\angle c = 180 - 40 = 140°$

$m\angle d = 40°$

$\boldsymbol{\angle a \cong \angle b}$

3. Use the two sets of linear angles to find *b* and then *c*.

$a = b$

$a + b + 70 = 180$

$2a + 70 = 180$

$a = b = 55°$

$b + c = 180°$

$55 + c = 180$

$c = \mathbf{125°}$

4. **C) is correct.** Use the formula for the volume of a sphere to find its radius.

$V = \frac{4}{3}\pi r^3$

$972\pi = \frac{4}{3}\pi r^3$

$r = 9$

Use the super Pythagorean theorem to find the side of the cube.

$d^2 = a^2 + b^2 + c^2$

$18^2 = 3s^2$

$s \approx 10.4$

Use the length of the side to find the volume of the cube.

$V = s^3$

$V \approx (10.4)^3$

$\boldsymbol{V \approx 1{,}125}$

5. **D) is correct.** There are an infinite number of points with distance four from the origin, all of which lie on a circle centered at the origin with a radius of 4.

6. **A) is correct.** Corresponding angles in right triangles are not necessarily the same, so they do not have to be similar.

B) All spheres are similar.

C) Corresponding angles in 30–60–90 triangles are the same, so all 30–60–90 triangles are similar.

D) Corresponding angles in a square are all the same (90°), so all squares are similar.

7. $\boldsymbol{x = 128\pi}$ **is correct.**

Set up a proportion. Cube the scale factor when calculating volume.

$\frac{54\pi}{x} = \frac{3^3}{4^3}$

$\boldsymbol{x = 128\pi}$

8. $\boldsymbol{32\pi}$ **ft.³ is correct.** Find the height of the cylinder using the equation for surface area.

$SA = 2\pi rh + 2\pi r^2$

$48\pi = 2\pi(4)h + 2\pi(4)^2$

$h = 2$

Find the volume using the volume equation.

$V = \pi r^2 h$

$V = \pi(4)^2(2) =$ **32π ft.^{3}**

CHAPTER FOUR

Data Analysis and Statistics

Describing Sets of Data

MEASURES of CENTRAL TENDENCY

Measures of central tendency help identify the center, or most typical, value within a data set. There are three such central tendencies that describe the "center" of the data in different ways. The **MEAN** is the arithmetic average and is found by dividing the sum of all measurements by the number of measurements. The mean of a population is written as μ and the mean of a sample is written as $\bar{x}$.

$$\text{population mean} = \mu = \frac{x_1 + x_2 + \ldots xN}{N} = \frac{\Sigma x}{N}$$

$$\text{sample mean} = \bar{x} = \frac{x_1 + x_2 + \ldots xn}{n} = \frac{\Sigma x}{n}$$

The data points are represented by x's with subscripts; the sum is denoted using the Greek letter sigma (Σ); N is the number of data points in the entire population; and n is the number of data points in a sample set.

The **MEDIAN** divides the measurements into two equal halves. The median is the measurement right in the middle of an odd set of measurements or the average of the two middle numbers in an even data set. When calculating the median, it is important to order the data values from least to greatest before attempting to locate the middle value. The **MODE** is simply the measurement that occurs most often. There can be many modes in a data set, or no mode. Since measures of central tendency describe a *center* of the data, all three of these measures will be between the lowest and highest data values (inclusive).

DID YOU KNOW?

When the same value is added to each term in a set, the mean increases by that value and the standard deviation is unchanged.

When each term in a set is multiplied by the same value, both the mean and standard deviation will also be multiplied by that value.

Unusually large or small values, called **OUTLIERS**, will affect the mean of a sample more than the mode. If there is a high outlier, the mean will be greater than the median; if there is a low outlier, the mean will be lower than the median. When outliers are present, the median is a better measure of the data's center than the mean because the median will be closer to the terms in the data set.

EXAMPLES

1. What is the mean of the following data set? {1000, 0.1, 10, 1}

2. What is the median of the following data set? {1000, 10, 1, 0.1}

3. Josey has an average of 81 on four equally weighted tests she has taken in her statistics class. She wants to determine what grade she must receive on her fifth test so that her mean is 83, which will give her a B in the course, but she does not remember her other scores. What grade must she receive on her fifth test?

MEASURES of VARIATION

The values in a data set can be very close together (close to the mean), or very spread out. This is called the **SPREAD** or **DISPERSION** of the data. There are a few **MEASURES OF VARIATION** (or **MEASURES OF DISPERSION**) that quantify the spread within a data set. **RANGE** is the difference between the largest and smallest data points in a set:

$$R = \textit{largest data point} - \textit{smallest data point}$$

Notice range depends on only two data points (the two extremes). Sometimes these data points are outliers; regardless, for a large data set, relying on only two data points is not an exact tool.

The understanding of the data set can be improved by calculating **QUARTILES.** To calculate quartiles, first arrange the data in ascending order and find the set's median (also called quartile 2 or Q2). Then find the median of the lower half of the data, called quartile 1 (Q1), and the median of the upper half of the data, called quartile 3 (Q3). These three points divide the data into four equal groups of data (thus the word *quartile*). Each quartile contains 25% of the data.

INTERQUARTILE RANGE (IQR) provides a more reliable range that is not as affected by extremes. IQR is the difference between the third quartile data point and the first quartile data point and gives the spread of the middle 50% of the data:

$$IQR = Q_3 - Q_1$$

The **VARIANCE** of a data set is simply the square of the standard variation:

$$V = \sigma^2 = \frac{1}{N} \sum_{i=1}^{N} (x_i - \mu)^2$$

Variance measures how narrowly or widely the data points are distributed. A variance of zero means every data point is the same; a large variance means the data is widely spread out.

EXAMPLE

4. What are the range and interquartile range of the following set? {3, 9, 49, 64, 81, 100, 121, 144, 169}

Graphs, Charts, and Tables

PIE CHARTS

A pie chart simply states the proportion of each category within the whole. To construct a pie chart, the categories of a data set must be determined. The frequency of each category must be found and that frequency converted to a percent of the total. To draw the pie chart, determine the angle of each slice by multiplying the percentage by 360°.

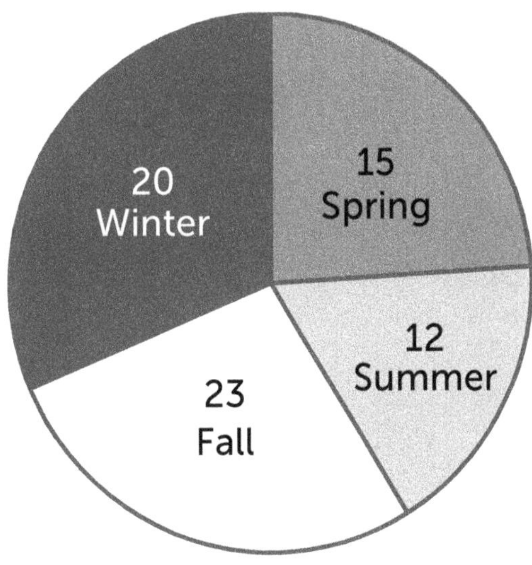

Figure 4.1. Pie Chart

EXAMPLE

5. A firm is screening applicants for a job by education-level attainment. There are 125 individuals in the pool: 5 have a doctorate, 20 have a master's degree, 40 have a bachelor's degree, 30 have an associate degree, and 30 have a high school degree. Construct a pie chart showing the highest level of education attained by the applicants.

SCATTER PLOTS

A scatter plot is displayed in the first quadrant of the xy-plane where all numbers are positive. Data points are plotted as ordered pairs, with one variable along the horizontal axis and the other along the vertical axis. Scatter plots can show if there is a correlation between two variables. There is a **POSITIVE CORRELATION** (expressed as a positive slope) if increasing one variable appears to result in an increase in the other variable. A **NEGATIVE CORRELATION** (expressed as a negative slope) occurs when an increase in one variable causes a decrease in the other. If the scatter plot shows no discernible pattern, then there is no correlation (a zero, mixed, or indiscernible slope).

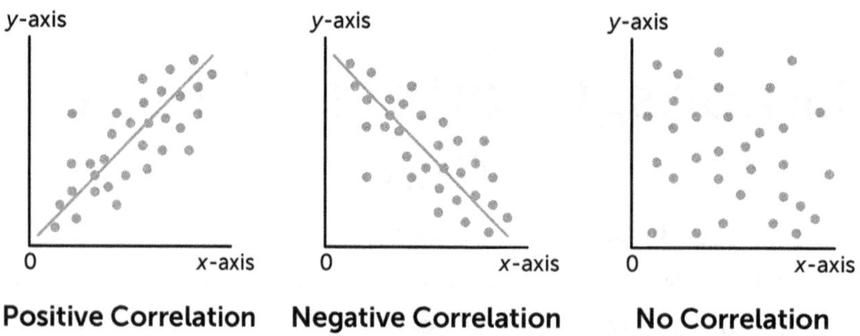

Figure 4.2. Scatter Plots and Correlation

Calculators or other software can be used to find the linear regression equation, which describes the general shape of the data. Graphing this equation produces the regression line, or line of best fit. The equation's **CORRELATION COEFFICIENT** (r) can be used to determine how closely the equation fits the data. The value of r is between –1 and 1. The closer r is to 1 (if the line has a positive slope) or –1 (if the line has a negative slope), the better the regression line fits the data. The closer the r value is to 0, the weaker the correlation between the line and the data. Generally, if the absolute value of the correlation coefficient is 0.8 or higher, then it is considered to be a strong correlation, while an $|r|$ value of less than 0.5 is considered a weak correlation.

To determine which curve is the "best fit" for a set of data, **RESIDUALS** are calculated. The calculator automatically calculates and saves these values to a list called RESID. These values are all the differences between the actual y-value of data points and the y-value calculated by the best-fit line or curve for that x-value. These values can be plotted on an xy-plane to produce a **RESIDUAL PLOT**. The residual plot helps determine if a line is the best model for the data. Residual points that are randomly dispersed above and below the horizontal indicate that a linear model is appropriate, while a u shape or upside-down u shape indicate a nonlinear model would be more appropriate.

Once a best-fit line is established, it can be used to estimate output values given an input value within the domain of the data. For a short extension outside that domain, reasonable predictions may be possible. However, the further from the domain of the data the line is extended, the greater the reduction in the accuracy of the prediction.

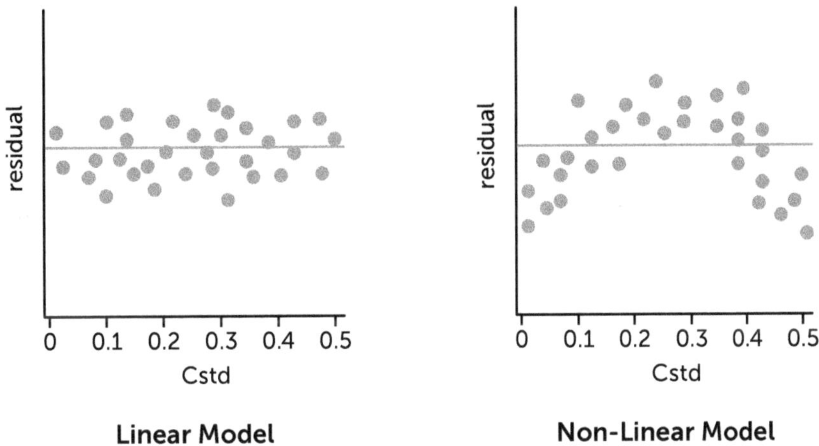

Figure 4.3. Residual Plots

It is important to note here that just because two variables have a strong positive or negative correlation, it cannot necessarily be inferred that those two quantities have a *causal* relationship—that is, that one variable changing *causes* the other quantity to change. There are often other factors that play into their relationship. For example, a positive correlation can be found between the number of ice cream sales and the number of shark attacks at a beach. It would be incorrect to say that selling more ice cream *causes* an increase in shark attacks. It is much more likely that on hot days more ice cream is sold, and many more people are swimming, so one of them is more likely to get attacked by a shark. Confusing correlation and causation is one of the most common statistical errors people make.

DID YOU KNOW?

A graphing calculator can provide the regression line, *r* value, and residuals list.

EXAMPLE

6. **Based on the scatter plot on the following page, where the *x*-axis represents hours spent studying per week and the *y*-axis represents the average percent grade on exams during the school year, is there a correlation between the amount of studying for a test and test results?**

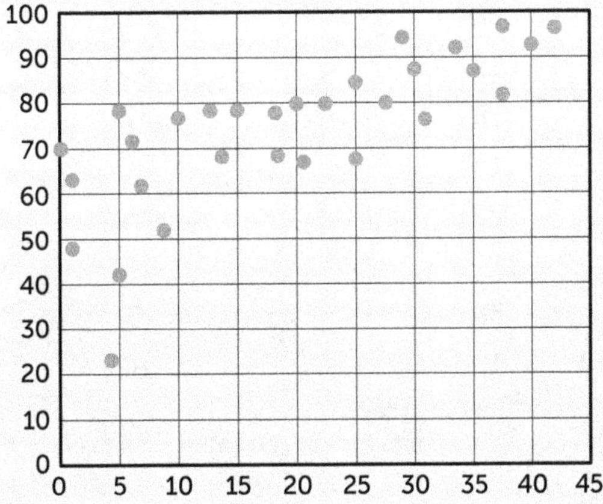

LINE GRAPHS

Line graphs are used to display a relationship between two variables, such as change over time. Like scatter plots, line graphs exist in quadrant I of the xy-plane. Line graphs are constructed by graphing each point and connecting each point to the next consecutive point by a line. To create a line graph, it may be necessary to consolidate data into single bivariate data points. Thus, a line graph is a function, with each x-value having exactly one y-value, whereas a scatter plot may have multiple y-values for one x-value.

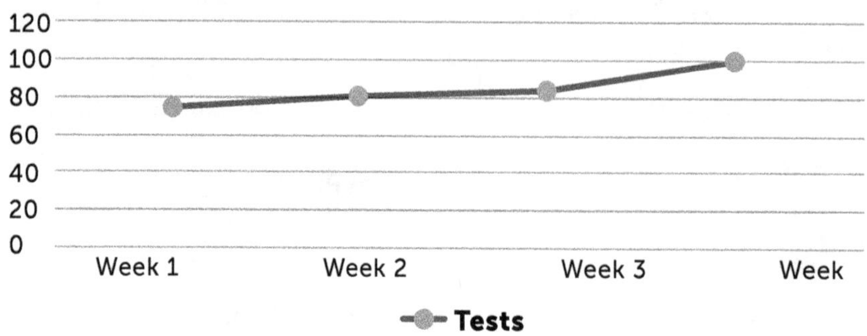

Figure 4.4. Line Graph

EXAMPLE

7. Create a line graph based on the following survey values, where the first column represents an individual's age and the other represents that individual's reported happiness level on a 20-point scale (0 being the least happy that person has been and 20 being the happiest). Then interpret the resulting graph to determine whether the following statement is true or false: *On average, middle-aged people are less happy than young or older people are.*

Age	Happiness	Age (continued)	Happiness (continued)
12	16	33	10
13	15	44	8
20	18	55	10
15	12	80	10
40	5	15	13
17	17	40	8
18	18	17	15
19	15	18	17
42	7	19	20
70	17	22	16
45	10	27	15
60	12	36	9
63	15	33	10
22	14	44	6
27	15		

BAR GRAPHS

Bar graphs compare differences between categories or changes over a time. The data is grouped into categories or ranges and represented by rectangles. A bar graph's rectangles can be vertical or horizontal, depending on whether the dependent variable is placed on the x- or y-axis. Instead of the xy-plane, however, one axis is made up of categories (or ranges) instead of a numeric scale. Bar graphs are useful because the differences between categories are easy to see: the height or length of each bar shows the value for each category.

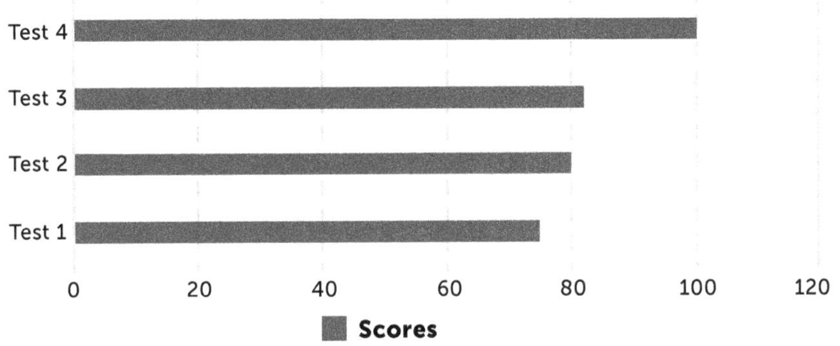

Figure 4.5. Bar Graph

EXAMPLE

8. A company X had a profit of $10,000 in 2010, $12,000 in 2011, $15,600 in 2012, and $20,280 in 2013. Create a bar graph displaying the profit from each of these four years.

STEM-and-LEAF PLOTS

Stem-and-leaf plots are ways of organizing large amounts of data by grouping it into classes. All data points are broken into two parts: a stem and a leaf. For instance, the number 512 might be broken into a stem of 5 and a leaf of 12. All data in the 500 range would appear in the same row (this group of data is a class). Usually a simple key is provided to explain how the data is being represented. For instance, 5|12 = 512 would show that the stems are representing hundreds. The advantage of this display is that it shows general density and shape of the data in a compact display, yet all original data points are preserved and available. It is also easy to find medians and quartiles from this display.

Stem	Leaf
0	5
1	6, 7
2	8, 3, 6
3	4, 5, 9, 5, 5, 8, 5
4	7, 7, 7, 8
5	5, 4
6	0

Figure 4.6. Stem-and-Leaf Plot

EXAMPLE

9. The table gives the weights of wrestlers (in pounds) for a certain competition. What is the mean, median, and IQR of the data?

2	05, 22, 53, 40
3	07, 22, 29, 45, 89, 96, 98
4	10, 25, 34
6	21

Key: 2|05 = 205 pounds

FREQUENCY TABLES and HISTOGRAMS

The frequency of a particular data point is the number of times that data point occurs. Constructing a frequency table requires that the data or data classes be arranged in ascending order in one column and the frequency in another column.

A histogram is a graphical representation of a frequency table used to compare frequencies. A histogram is constructed in quadrant I of the *xy*-plane, with data in each equal-width class presented as a bar and the height of each bar representing the frequency of that class. Unlike bar graphs, histograms cannot have gaps between bars. A histogram is used to determine the distribution of data among the classes.

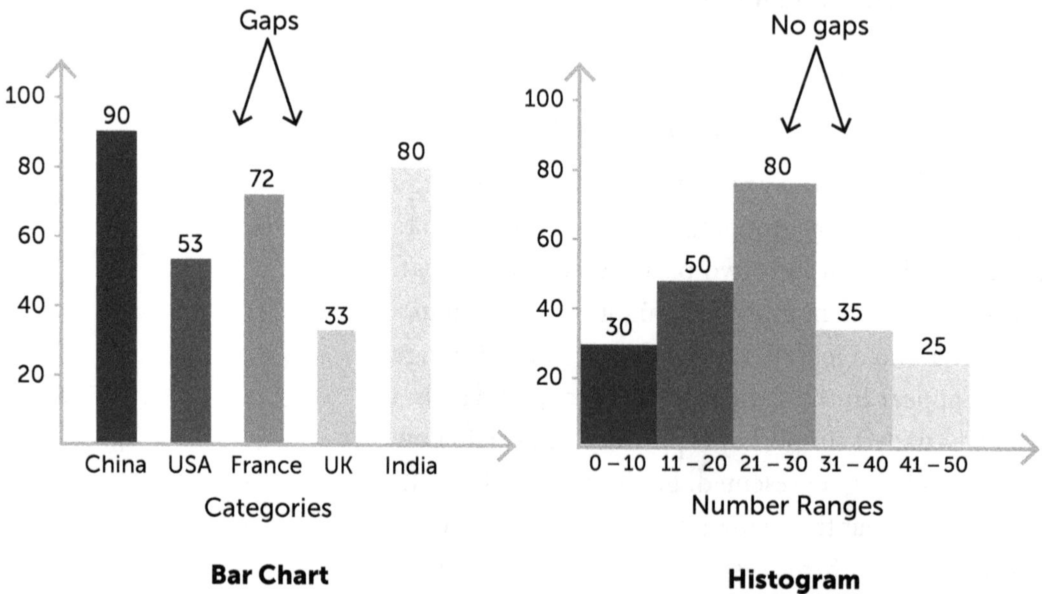

Figure 4.7. Bar Chart vs. Histogram

Histograms can be symmetrical, skewed left or right, or multimodal (data spread around). Note that **SKEWED LEFT** means the peak of the data is on the *right*, with a tail to the left, while **SKEWED RIGHT** means the peak is on the *left*, with a tail to the right. This seems counterintuitive to many; the "left" or "right" always refers to the tail of the data. This is because a long tail to the right, for example, means there are high outlier values that are skewing the data to the right.

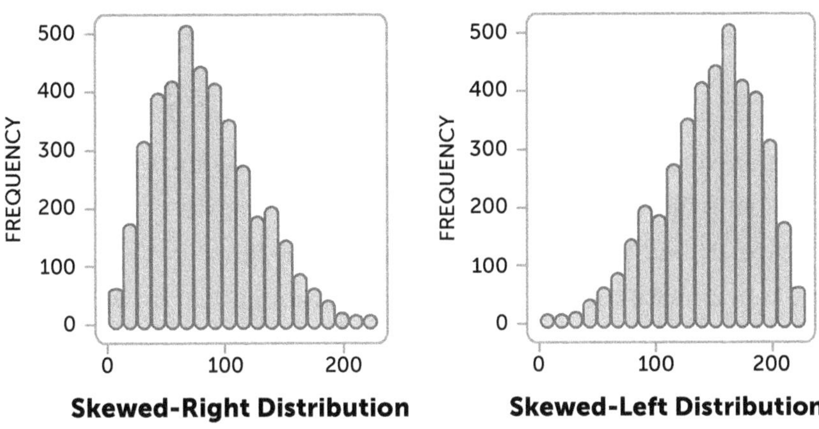

Figure 4.8. Histrograms

A **TWO-WAY FREQUENCY TABLE** compares **CATEGORICAL DATA** (data in more than one category) of two related variables (bivariate data). Two-way frequency tables are also called **CONTINGENCY TABLES** and are often used to analyze survey results. One category is displayed along the top of the table and the other category down along the side. Rows and columns are added and the sums appear at the end of the row or column. The sum of all the row data must equal the sum of all the column data.

From a two-way frequency table, the **JOINT RELATIVE FREQUENCY** of a particular category can be calculated by taking the number in the row and column of the categories in question and dividing by the total number surveyed. This gives the percent of the total in that particular category. Sometimes the **CONDITIONAL RELATIVE FREQUENCY** is of interest. In this case, calculate the relative frequency confined to a single row or column.

Students by Grade and Gender					
	9th Grade	10th Grade	11th Grade	12th Grade	Total
Male	57	63	75	61	256
Female	54	42	71	60	227
Total	111	105	146	121	483

Figure 4.9. Two-Way Frequency Table

EXAMPLES

10. Cineflix movie theater polled its moviegoers on a weeknight to determine their favorite type of movie. The results are in the two-way frequency table below.

Moviegoers	Comedy	Action	Horror	Totals
Male	15	24	21	60
Female	8	18	17	43
Totals	23	42	38	103

Determine whether each of the following statements is true or false.

A) Action films are the most popular type of movie

B) About 1 in 5 moviegoers prefers comedy films

C) Men choose the horror genre more frequently than women do

11. A café owner tracked the number of customers he had over a twelve-hour period in the following frequency table. Display the data in a histogram and determine what kind of distribution there is in the data.

Time	Number of Customers
6 a.m. – 8 a.m.	5
8 a.m. – 9 a.m.	6
9 a.m. – 10 a.m.	5
10 a.m. – 12 p.m.	23
12 p.m. – 2 p.m.	24
2 p.m. – 4 p.m.	9
4 p.m. – 6 p.m.	4

Test Your Knowledge

Work the problem, and then choose the most correct answer.

Use the following graph for questions 1 and 2.

Number of Months with 3 or Fewer Than 3 Inches of Rain

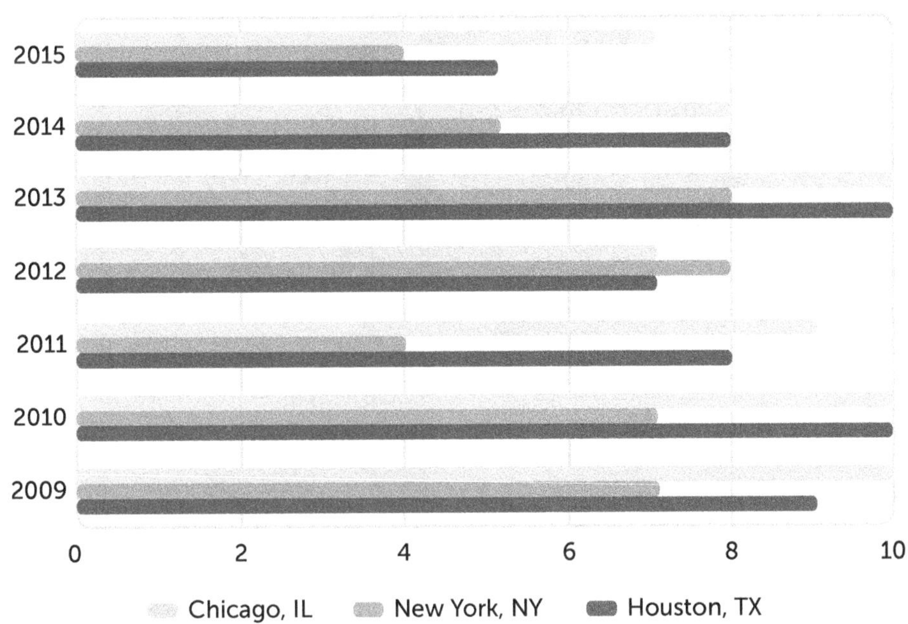

1. New York had the fewest months with less than 3 inches of rain in every year except:
   A) 2012
   B) 2013
   C) 2014
   D) 2015

2. From 2009 to 2015, what is the average number of months that Chicago had 3 or less inches of rain?
   A) 6
   B) 7
   C) 8
   D) 9

3. What is the relationship between the mean and the median in a data set that is skewed right?
   A) The mean is greater than the median.
   B) The mean is less than the median.
   C) The mean and median are equal.
   D) The mean may be greater than, less than, or equal to the median.

4. A homeowner is looking to put a pool in her backyard. The homeowner learns the average cost for such a project in her area is $20,000. If the homeowner wants to know how much prices may vary from the average, what measurement should she find?
   A) range
   B) interquartile range
   C) standard deviation
   D) quartiles

5. What is the approximate standard deviation of the given set?

{5, 8, 22, 23, 27, 35, 35, 60, 61, 67}

A) 21.9

B) 25.3

C) ≈ 34.3

D) ≈ 480.7

6. Danny collects coins. The table shows how many of each type of coin Danny collects for 4 days. Which statement is true?

Danny's Coin Collection

Coin	Day 1	Day 2	Day 3	Day 4
Pennies	1	4	5	1
Nickels	4	3	2	5
Dimes	3	2	2	3
Quarters	0	5	4	1

A. The mean number of nickels is greater than the mean number of quarters.

B. The mean number of quarters is greater than the mean number of pennies.

C. The range of dimes is greater than the range of quarters.

D. The median number of pennies is 5.

7. The mean of 13 numbers is 30. The mean of 8 of these numbers is 42. What is the mean of the other 5 numbers?

A) 5.5

B) 10.8

C) 16.4

D) 21.2

8. What is the difference between the range and the interquartile range of the following set?

$\left\{\frac{1}{20}, \frac{1}{16}, \frac{1}{14}, \frac{1}{12}, \frac{1}{10}, \frac{1}{8}, \frac{1}{6}, \frac{1}{4}, \frac{1}{2}\right\}$

A) $\frac{9}{20}$

B) $\frac{15}{24}$

C) $\frac{95}{672}$

D) $\frac{1037}{3360}$

Answer Key

EXAMPLES

1. Use the equation to find the mean of a sample:

$$\frac{1000 + 0.1 + 10 + 1}{4} = \mathbf{252.78}$$

2. Since there are an even number of data points in the set, the median will be the mean of the two middle numbers. Order the numbers from least to greatest: 0.1, 1, 10, and 1000. The two middle numbers are 1 and 10, and their mean is:

$$\frac{1 + 10}{2} = \mathbf{5.5}$$

3. Even though Josey does not know her test scores, she knows her average. Therefore it can be assumed that each test score was 81, since four scores of 81 would average to 81. To find the score, *x*, that she needs use the equation for the mean of a sample:

$$\frac{4(81) + x}{5} = 83$$

$$324 + x = 415$$

$$\boldsymbol{x = 91}$$

4. Use the equation for range.

R = largest point – smallest point = 169 – 3 = **166**

Place the terms in numerical order and identify Q1, Q2, and Q3.

3

9

$\rightarrow Q1 = \frac{49 + 9}{2} = 29$

49

64

81 → Q2

100

121

$\rightarrow Q3 = \frac{121 + 144}{2} = 132.5$

144

169

Find the IQR by subtracting Q1 from Q3.

IQR = Q3 – Q1 = 132.5 – 29 = **103.5**

5. Create a frequency table to find the percentages and angle measurement for each category.

Category	Frequency	Percent	Angle Measure
High School	30	24%	86.4
Associate	30	24%	86.4
Bachelor's	40	32%	115.2
Master's	20	16%	57.6
Doctorate	5	4%	14.4

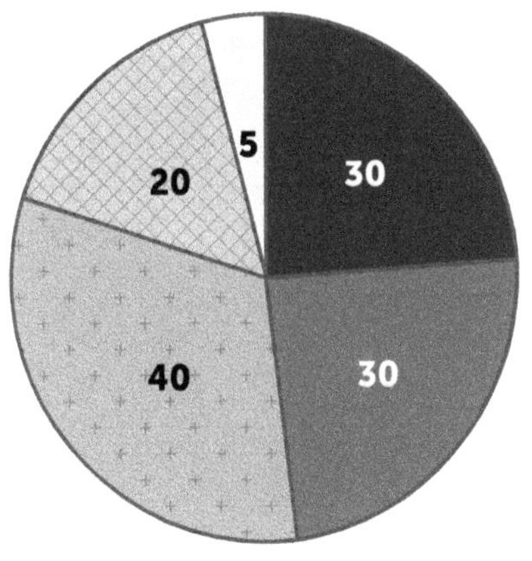

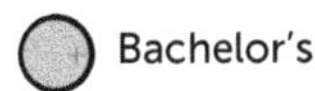

6. There is a somewhat weak positive correlation. As the number of hours spent studying increases, the average percent grade also generally increases.

7. To construct a line graph, the data must be ordered into consolidated categories by averaging the data of people who have the same age so that the data is one-to-one. For example, there are 2 twenty-two-year-olds who are reporting. Their average happiness level is 15. When all the data has been consolidated and ordered from least to greatest, the table and graph below can be presented.

Age	Happiness
12	16
13	15
15	12.5
17	16
18	17.5
19	17.5
20	18
22	15
27	15
33	10
36	10.5
40	6.5
42	7
44	7
45	10
55	10
60	12
63	15
70	17
80	10

The statement that, on average, middle-aged people are less happy than young or older people appears to be true. According to the graph, people in their thirties, forties, and fifties are less happy than people in their teens, twenties, sixties, and seventies.

8. Place years on the independent axis, and profit on the dependent axis, and then draw a box showing the profit for each year.

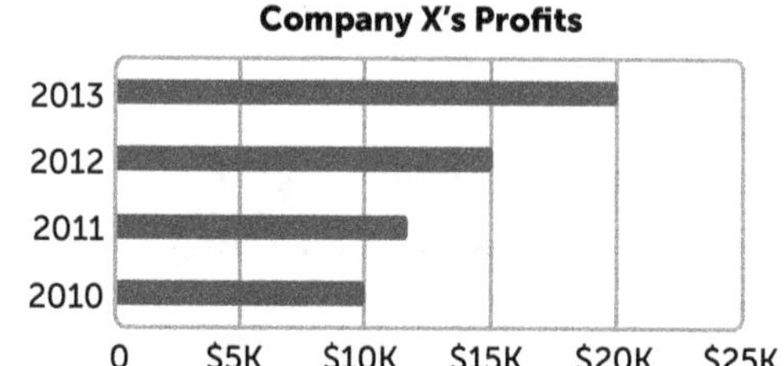

9. Find the mean using the equation for the population mean.

$\mu = \frac{\Sigma x}{N} = \frac{5281}{15} = \mathbf{353.1\ lbs.}$

Find the median and IQR by counting the leaves and identifying Q1, Q2, and Q3.

Q1 = 253

Q2 = 345

Q3 = 410

IQR = 410 – 253 = 157

The median is 345 lbs. The IQR is 157 lbs.

10. **A) True.** More people (42) chose action movies than comedy (23) or horror (38).

B) True. Find the ratio of total number of people who prefer comedy to total number of people. $\frac{23}{103}$ = 0.22; 1 in 5 is 20%, so 22% is about the same.

C) False. The percentage of men who choose horror is less than the percentage of women who do.

part = number of men who prefer horror =21

whole = number of men surveyed = 60

percent = $\frac{\text{part}}{\text{whole}} = \frac{21}{60}$
= 0.35 = 35%

part = number of women who prefer horror =17

whole = number of women surveyed = 43

percent = $\frac{\text{part}}{\text{whole}} = \frac{17}{43}$
= 0.40 = 40%

11. Since time is the independent variable, it is on the x-axis and the number of customers is on the y-axis. For the histogram to correctly display data continuously, categories on the x-axis must be equal 2-hour segments. The 8 a.m. – 9 a.m. and 9 a.m. – 10 a.m. categories must be combined for a total of 11 customers in that time period. Although not perfectly symmetrical, the amount of customers peaks in the middle and is therefore considered symmetrical.

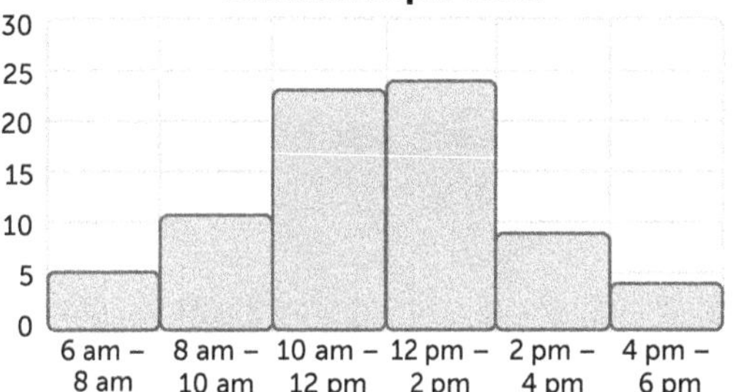

TEST YOUR KNOWLEDGE

1. **A) is correct.** In 2012, New York had more months with less than 3 inches of rain than either Chicago or Houston.

2. **D) is correct.** Use the graph to find the number of months Chicago had less than 3 inches of rain year, and then find the average.

   months with < 3 inches rain in Chicago: {7, 8, 10, 7, 9, 10, 10}

   $\frac{(7 + 8 + 10 + 7 + 9 + 10 + 1)}{7} = 8.7 \approx \mathbf{9}$

3. **A) is correct.** If the data is skewed right, the set includes extremes values that are to the right, or high. The median is unaffected by these high values, but the mean includes these high values and would therefore be greater.

4. **C) is correct.** Standard deviation describes the average distance between data points and the mean. Quartiles, range, and interquartile range do not reference the mean.

5. **A) is correct.** Use the formula for standard deviation.

   $s = \sqrt{\frac{\sum(x_i - x)^2}{n - 1}}$

   $x = \frac{5 + 8 + 22 + 23 + 27 + 35 + 35 + 60 + 61 + 67}{10}$

   $= 34.3$

   $(5 - 34.3)^2 = (-29.3)^2 = 858.5$

   $(8 - 34.3)^2 = (-26.3)^2 = 691.7$

   $(22 - 34.3)^2 = (-12.3)^2 = 151.3$

   $(23 - 34.3)^2 = (-11.3)^2 = 127.7$

   $(27 - 34.3)^2 = (-7.3)^2 = 53.3$

   $(35 - 34.3)^2 = (0.7)^2 = 0.49$

   $(35 - 34.3)^2 = (0.7)^2 = 0.49$

   $(60 - 34.3)^2 = (25.7)^2 = 660.5$

   $(61 - 34.3)^2 = (26.7)^2 = 712.9$

   $(67 - 34.3)^2 = (32.7)^2 = 1069.3$

   $\sum(x_i - x)^2 = 4326.2$

   $s = \sqrt{\frac{4326.2}{10 - 1}}$

   $= \sqrt{480.7}$

   $= \mathbf{21.9}$

6. **A) is true.**

   mean number of nickels = $\frac{(4 + 3 + 2 + 2)}{4} = \frac{11}{4}$ = 2.75 nickles

   mean number of quarters = $\frac{(0 + 5 + 4 + 1)}{4} = \frac{10}{4}$ = 2.5 quarters

B) is false

mean number of pennies = $\frac{(1 + 4 + 5 + 1)}{4} = \frac{11}{4}$ = 2.75 pennies

mean number of quarters = 2.5 quarters

C) is false.

range of dimes = 3 – 2 = 1

range of quarters = 5 – 0 = 5

D) is false.

pennies = {1, 1, 4, 5}

median of pennies = $\frac{(1+ 4)}{2}$ = 2.5

7. **B) is correct.** Find the sum of the 13 numbers whose mean is 30.

   13 × 30 = 390

   Find the sum of the 8 numbers whose mean is 42.

   8 × 42 = 336

   Find the sum and mean of the remaining 5 numbers.

   390 – 336 = 54

   $\frac{54}{5}$ = **10.8**

8. **D) is correct.** Find the range and the interquartile range, and then find the difference.

   $R = \frac{1}{2} - \frac{1}{20} = \frac{9}{20}$

   $Q1 = \frac{15}{224}$

   $Q3 = \frac{5}{24}$

   $IQR = \frac{5}{24} - \frac{15}{224} = \frac{95}{672}$

   $\frac{9}{20} - \frac{95}{672} = \mathbf{\frac{1037}{3360}}$

CHAPTER FIVE

Logic and Probability

Logic and Set Theory

LOGIC

Mathematical logic is a systematic method of determining the truth of a **PROPOSITION**, or statement. A proposition can be true or false, a label called the proposition's **TRUTH VALUE.** In the context of logical arguments, a statement cannot be both true and false; it also cannot be neither true nor false. Propositions are represented by variables, usually p, q, or r.

A **NEGATION** has the opposite truth value of the original statement, and is often denoted by the symbol tilde (~). The statement $\sim p$ is read as "not p." Examples of statements and their negations are below. Note that $\sim p$ is not necessarily false; it is simply the opposite of p.

- p: 4 is an even number (true)
  $\sim p$: 4 is not an even number (false)
- p: Dogs lay eggs (false)
  $\sim p$: Dogs do not lay eggs (true)

A **TRUTH TABLE** shows all the possible inputs and truth output values of a statement or proposition. These tables are constructed by writing the variables for each statement and operation across the top row, and then listing all possible true/false values in the columns. In the table below, the statement p and its negation are in the top row, and the possible true/false values for p are in the left column. The right column ($\sim p$) can then be filled in.

p	**~p**
T	F
F	T

Figure 5.1. Truth Table

A **CONJUNCTION** between two variables or statements is an *and* statement. It is true only when both variables or statements are true. For all other situations, the result is false. A conjunction between statements p and q is written $p \wedge q$.

p	q	$p \wedge q$
T	T	T
T	F	F
F	T	F
F	F	F

Figure 5.2. Conjunction

A **DISJUNCTION** between two variables or statements is an inclusive *or* statement, and is denoted $p \vee q$. This statement is true whenever p is true, q is true, or both are true.

An **IMPLICATION** statement is an *if... then* statement. The statement "if p, then q" is also written as $p \to q$. The implication statement is false only when the first proposition is true and the second is false:

The **BICONDITIONAL** or **EQUIVALENCE** statement is true whenever both p and q have the same truth value:

p	q	$p \vee q$
T	T	T
T	F	T
F	T	T
F	F	F

Figure 5.3. Disjunction

p	q	$p \to q$
T	T	T
T	F	F
F	T	T
F	F	F

Figure 5.4. Implication

p	q	$p \leftrightarrow q$
T	T	T
T	F	F
F	T	F
F	F	T

Figure 5.5. Bioconditional

Truth tables can be used to show that two statements are logically equivalent by showing that they have the same truth values under all circumstances. For example, a truth table can prove that the implication statement $p \to q$ and the contrapositive of that statement $\sim q \to \sim p$ are equivalent. To construct the table, create columns for p and q, and fill these with all possible true/false combinations. Next, create columns for each operation and find its truth value. Because the columns for $p \to q$ and $\sim q \to \sim p$ are identical, the statements are equivalent.

p	q	$\sim p$	$\sim q$	$p \to q$	$\sim q \to \sim p$
T	T	F	F	T	T
T	F	F	T	F	F
F	T	T	F	T	T
F	F	T	T	T	T

Figure 5.6. Truth Table with Two Statements

EXAMPLE

1. Prove De Morgan's theorem $\sim(p \vee q) = \sim p \wedge \sim q$ using a truth table.

SET THEORY

A **SET** is any collection of items. In mathematics, a set is represented by a capital letter and described inside curly brackets. For example, if S is the set of all integers less than 10, then $S = \{x|x \text{ is an integer and } x < 10\}$. The vertical bar | is read *such that*. The set that contains no elements is called the **EMPTY SET** or the **NULL SET** and is denoted by empty brackets { } or the symbol ∅.

DID YOU KNOW?

The notation $x \in A$ is read as "x is an element of A."

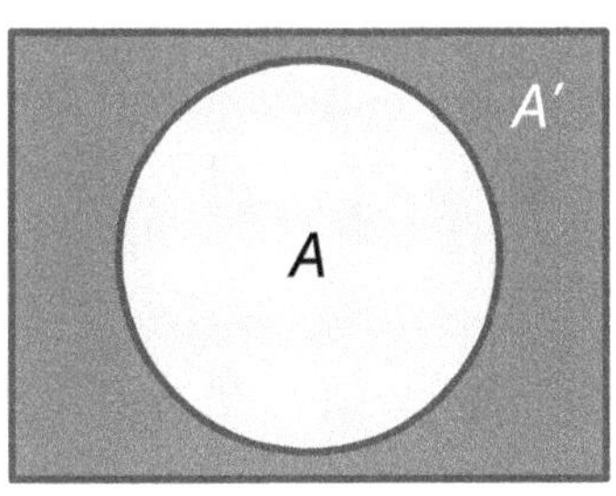

Figure 5.7. Venn Diagram

Usually there is a larger set that any specific problem is based in, called the **UNIVERSAL SET** or **U**. For example, in the set S described above, the universal set might be the set of all real numbers. The **COMPLEMENT** of set A, denoted by $\overline{A}$ or A', is the set of all items in the universal set, but NOT in A. It can be helpful when working with sets to represent them with a **VENN DIAGRAM**.

Oftentimes, the task will be working with multiple sets: A, B, C, etc. A **UNION** between two sets means that the data in both sets is combined into a single, larger set. The union of two sets, denoted $A \cup B$ contains all the data that is in either set A or set B or both (called an **INCLUSIVE OR**). If $A = \{1, 4, 7\}$ and $B = \{2, 4, 5, 8\}$, then $A \cup B = \{1, 2, 4, 5, 7, 8\}$ (notice 4 is included only once). The **INTERSECTION** of two sets, denoted $A \cap B$ includes only elements that are in both A and B. Thus, $A \cap B = \{4\}$ for the sets given above.

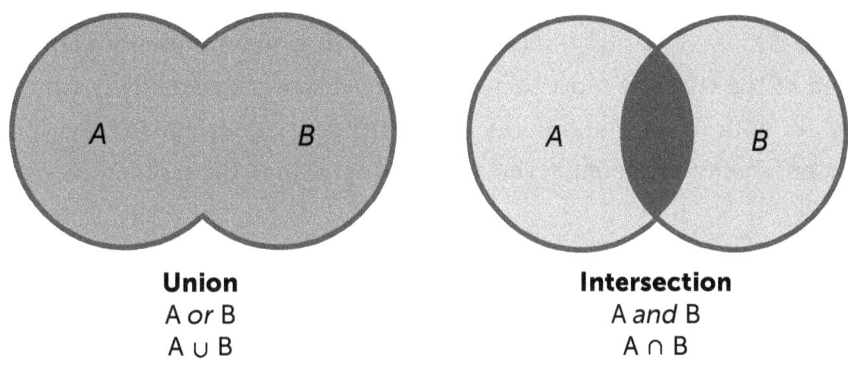

Figure 5.8. Unions and Intersections

If there is no common data in the sets in question, then the intersection is the null set. Two sets that have no elements in common (and thus have a null in the intersection set) are said to be **DISJOINT**. The **DIFFERENCE** $\boldsymbol{B - A}$ or **RELATIVE COMPLEMENT** between two sets is the set of all the values that are in B, but not in A. For the sets defined above, $B - A = \{2, 5, 8\}$ and $A - B = \{1, 7\}$. The relative complement is sometimes denoted as $\boldsymbol{B \backslash A}$.

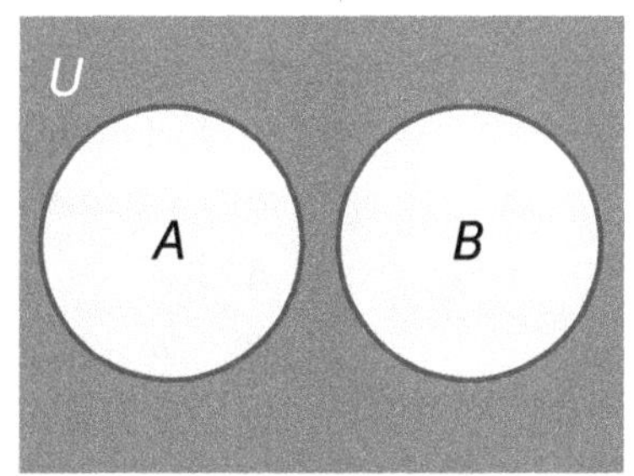

Figure 5.9. Disjoint Sets

Mathematical tasks often involve working with multiple sets. Just like numbers, sets and set operations have identities and properties.

Set Identities

$A \cup \varnothing = A$	$A \cup U = U$	$A \cup \overline{A} = U$
$A \cap \varnothing = A$	$A \cap U = A$	$A \cap \overline{A} = \varnothing$

Set Properties

Commutative Property	$A \cup B = B \cup A$	$A \cap B = B \cap A$
Associative Property	$A \cup (B \cup C) = (A \cup B) \cup C$	$A \cap (B \cap C) = (A \cap B) \cap C$
Distributive Property	$A \cup (B \cap C) = (A \cup B) \cap (A \cup C)$	$A \cap (B \cup C) = (A \cap B) \cup (A \cap C)$

De Morgan's Laws

$\overline{(A \cup B)} = \overline{A} \cap \overline{B}$	$\overline{(A \cap B)} = \overline{(A \cup B)}$

The number of elements in a set A is denoted $n(A)$. For the set A above, $n(A) = 3$, since there are three elements in that set. The number of elements in the union of two sets is $n(A \cup B) = n(A) + n(B) - n(A \cap B)$. Note that the number of elements in the intersection of the two sets must be subtracted because they are being counted twice, since they are both in set A and in set B. The number of elements in the complement of A is the number of elements in the universal set minus the number in set A: $n(\overline{A}) = n(U) - n(A)$.

It is helpful to note here how similar set theory is to the logic operators of the previous section: negation corresponds to complements, the "and" ($\wedge$) operator to intersection ($\cap$), and the "or" ($\vee$) operator to unions ($\cup$); notice even the symbols are similar.

EXAMPLES

2. Suppose the universal set U is the set of all integers between −10 and 10 inclusive. If $A = \{x \in U | x \text{ is a multiple of } 5\}$ and $B = \{x \in U | x \text{ is a multiple of } 2\}$ are subsets within the universal set, find $\overline{A}$, $A \cup B$ and $A \cap B$, and $\overline{A}$, $A \cap B$.

A. $\overline{A}$

B. $A \cup B$

C. $A \cap B$

D. $\overline{A} \cap \overline{B}$

3. Construct a Venn diagram depicting the intersection, if any, of $Y=\{x \mid x \text{ is an integer and } 0 < x < 9\}$ and $Z = \{-4, 0, 4, 8, 12, 16\}$.

Probability

Probability describes how likely something is to happen. In probability, an **EVENT** is the single result of a trial, and an **OUTCOME** is a possible event that results from a trial. The collection of all possible outcomes for a particular trial is called the **SAMPLE SPACE.** For example, when rolling a die, the sample space is the numbers 1 – 6. Rolling a single number, such as 4, would be a single event.

COUNTING PRINCIPLES

Counting principles are methods used to find the number of possible outcomes for a given situation. The **FUNDAMENTAL COUNTING PRINCIPLE** states that, for a series of independent events, the number of outcomes can be found by multiplying the number of possible outcomes for each event. For example, if a die is rolled (6 possible outcomes) and a coin is tossed (2 possible outcomes), there are $6 \times 2 = 12$ total possible outcomes.

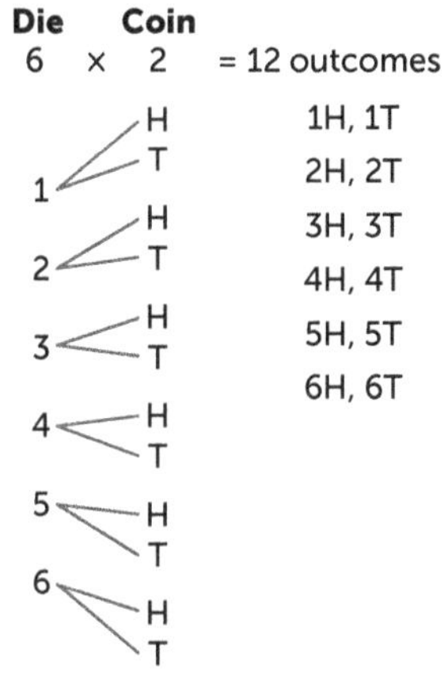

Die Coin
6 × 2 = 12 outcomes
1H, 1T
2H, 2T
3H, 3T
4H, 4T
5H, 5T
6H, 6T

Figure 5.10. Fundamental Counting Principle

Combinations and permutations describe how many ways a number of objects taken from a group can be arranged. The number of objects in the group is written n, and the number of objects to be arranged is represented by r (or k). In a **COMBINATION**, the order of the selections does not matter because every available slot to be filled is the same. Examples of combinations include:

- picking 3 people from a group of 12 to form a committee (220 possible committees)
- picking 3 pizza toppings from 10 options (120 possible pizzas)

In a **PERMUTATION**, the order of the selection matters, meaning each available slot is different. Examples of permutations include:

- handing out gold, silver, and bronze medals in a race with 100 participants (970,200 possible combinations)
- selecting a president, vice-president, secretary, and treasurer from among a committee of 12 people (11,880 possible combinations)

The formulas for the both calculations are similar. The only difference—the $r!$ in the denominator of a combination—accounts for redundant outcomes. Note that both permutations and combinations can be written in several different shortened notations.

$$\text{Permutation: } P(n,r) = {}_nP_r = \frac{n!}{(n-r)!}$$

$$\text{Combination: } C(n,r) = nCr = \binom{n}{r} = \frac{n!}{(n-r)!r!}$$

EXAMPLES

4. A personal assistant is struggling to pick a shirt, tie, and cufflink set that go together. If his client has 70 shirts, 2 ties, and 5 cufflinks, how many possible combinations does he have to consider?

5. If there are 20 applicants for 3 open positions, in how many different ways can a team of 3 be hired?

6. Calculate the number of unique permutations that can be made with five of the letters in the word *pickle*.

7. Find the number of permutations that can be made out of all the letters in the word *cheese*.

PROBABILITY of a SINGLE EVENT

The probability of a single event occurring is the number of outcomes in which that event occurs (called **FAVORABLE EVENTS**) divided by the number of items in the sample space (total possible outcomes):

$$P(\text{an event}) = \frac{\textit{number of favorable outcomes}}{\textit{total number of possible outcomes}}$$

The probability of any event occurring will always be a fraction or decimal between 0 and 1. It may also be expressed as a percent. An event with 0 probability will never occur and an event with a probability of 1 is certain to occur. The probability of an event not occurring is referred to as that event's **COMPLEMENT**. The sum of an event's probability and the probability of that event's complement will always be 1.

EXAMPLES

8. What is the probability that an even number results when a six-sided die is rolled? What is the probability the die lands on 5?

9. Only 20 tickets were issued in a raffle. If someone were to buy 6 tickets, what is the probability that person would not win the raffle?

10. A bag contains 26 tiles representing the 26 letters of the English alphabet. If 3 tiles are drawn from the bag without replacement, what is the probability that all 3 will be consonants?

PROBABILITY of MULTIPLE EVENTS

If events are **INDEPENDENT**, the probability of one occurring does not affect the probability of the other event occurring. Rolling a die and getting one number does not change the probability of getting any particular number on the next roll. The number of faces has not changed, so these are independent events.

If events are **DEPENDENT**, the probability of one occurring changes the probability of the other event occurring. Drawing a card from a deck without replacing it will affect the probability of the next card drawn because the number of available cards has changed.

DID YOU KNOW?
When drawing objects, the phrase *with replacement* describes independent events, and *without replacement* describes dependent events.

To find the probability that two or more independent events will occur (A and B), simply multiply the probabilities of each individual event together. To find the probability that one, the other, or both will occur (A or B), it's necessary to add their probabilities and then subtract their overlap (which prevents the same values from being counted twice).

CONDITIONAL PROBABILITY is the probability of an event occurring given that another event has occurred. The notation $P(B|A)$ represents the probability that event B occurs, given that event A has already occurred (it is read "probability of B, given A").

Table 5.1. Probability Formulas

Independent Events		Dependent Events
Intersection *and*	Union *or*	Conditional
$P(A \cap B) = P(A) \times P(B)$	$P(A \cup B) = P(A) + P(B) - P(A \cap B)$	$P(B\|A) = P(A \cap B)/P(A)$
A B	A B	A B|A

Two events that are **MUTUALLY EXCLUSIVE** CANNOT happen at the same time. This is similar to disjoint sets in set theory. The probability that two mutually exclusive events will occur is zero. **MUTUALLY INCLUSIVE** events share common outcomes.

EXAMPLES

11. A card is drawn from a standard 52 card deck. What is the probability that it is either a queen or a heart?

12. A group of ten individuals is drawing straws from a group of 28 long straws and 2 short straws. If the straws are not replaced, what is the probability, as a percentage, that neither of the first two individuals will draw a short straw?

BINOMIAL PROBABILITY

A binomial (or Bernoulli) trial is an experiment with exactly two mutually exclusive outcomes (often labeled success and failure) where the probability of each outcome is constant. The probability of success is given as p, and the probability of failure is $q = 1 - p$. The **BINOMIAL PROBABILITY** formula can be used to determine the probability of getting a certain number of successes (r) within a given number of trials (n). These values can also be used to find the expected value (μ), or mean, of the trial, and its standard deviation (σ).

$$P = {}_nC_r(p^r)(q^{n-r}) \qquad \mu = np \qquad \sigma = \sqrt{np(1-p)}$$

EXAMPLE

13. What is the probability of rolling a five on a standard 6-sided die 4 times in 10 tries?

Probability Distributions and Expected Value

RANDOM VARIABLES

A **RANDOM VARIABLE** is a variable whose value depends on a random event. Random variables are usually denoted with a capital X or Y. A random variable may be discrete or continuous. Discrete random variables have a finite number of specific possible outcomes. An example of a discrete random variable would be how many "heads" outcomes result when a coin is flipped three times. The distinct possible values for this variable would be 0, 1, 2, or 3, as either zero, one, two, or three heads would result upon three flips of a coin.

A **CONTINUOUS** random value is defined over an interval of values, and has infinitely many possible values. An example of a continuous random variable is the amount of time an airplane is delayed. There are many, many possible outcomes in this situation. Usually, if something is being measured (time, weight, height, etc.), the variable is continuous.

Once a random variable is assigned, it's possible to find the probability for each of the that variable's values. In the example of flipping a coin three times, let X be the random variable that represents how many "heads" outcomes result. Note that each of the four possible values for this random variable are NOT equally likely, even though the possibility of tossing a head or a tail is equally likely. The sample space of the experiment of flipping a coin three times is {HHH, HHT, HTH, HTT, THH, THT, TTH,

TTT}. The probabilities of random variable X taking each of its possible values can be displayed in a table. This is the **PROBABILITY DISTRIBUTION** for each value of X:

X:	0	1	2	3
$P(X)$:	0.125	0.375	0.375	0.125

This distribution also can be displayed graphically:

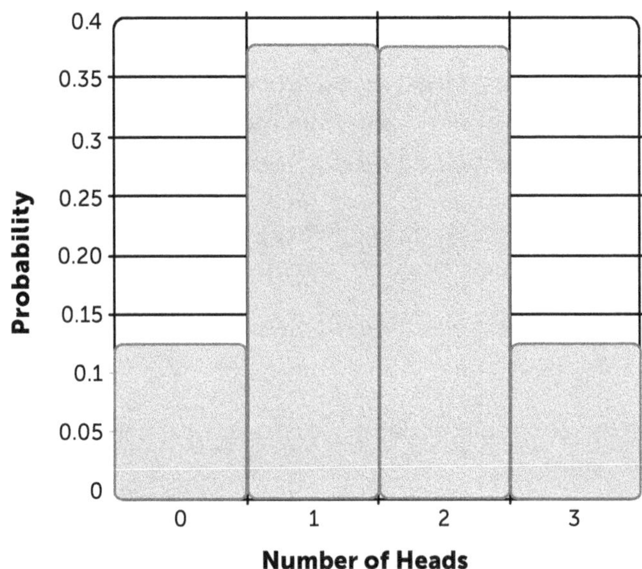

Figure 5.11. Probability Distribution

Notice that the sum of the probabilities is 1, as is the sum of the areas of the rectangles of the histogram. The sum of the probabilities of any random variable's output is always 1. Essentially, defining a random variable defines a function $P(X)$, the output of which are probabilities (making the range $0 \leq X \leq 1$), as a function of the random variable X; this is a **PROBABILITY DISTRIBUTION FUNCTION.**

Other probabilities also can be calculated using the above table. For example, to find the probability that either two or three heads occur, $P(X = 2 \text{ or } X = 3) = P(X = 2) + P(X = 3) = 0.375 + 0.125 = 0.5$. The probability that at least one head occurs is $1 - P(X = 0) = 1 - 0.125 = 0.875$ (using the complement rule).

For continuous random variables, the total area under the probability distribution curve will also be 1. Since the number of possible values taken on by a continuous random variable is infinite, the probability of any single value of X is 0. Instead, probabilities of intervals are calculated. These probabilities can be calculated by finding the area under the distribution curve (the integral) over that interval.

DID YOU KNOW?

Expected value can be used to weigh the possible outcomes of a decision by assigning probabilities to payoff values and determining which expected value is most beneficial.

The **EXPECTED VALUE**, $E(x)$, of a discrete random variable is the weighted average (or mean) of the variable. To calculate the expected value, calculate the sum of the products of each data point multiplied by the probability of that point. That is, for data points $x_1, x_2, x_3, \dots x_n$,

$$E(X) = \sum_{i=1}^{n} x_i P(x_i)$$

EXAMPLES

14. A bag contains 6 balls numbered 1 – 6. Two balls are removed from the bag, and the sum of the two balls is recorded. If this experiment is repeated 50 times, about how many times would the sum be 3? What would the average value of a roll be?

15. Suppose data is collected on the length of delays in the air travel industry. The following data are collected (data in minutes):

5	5	10	10	11	11	18	28	25	23	32	33	34
35	36	36	36	39	45	55	57	72	74	88	90	94

Determine the probability that if a customer experiences a delay, it will be less than 40 minutes.

THE NORMAL DISTRIBUTION

The **NORMAL DISTRIBUTION** or **NORMAL CURVE** is an example of a continuous probability distribution. The normal curve is a bell-shaped curve that occurs frequently in natural phenomena. Normal distributions are symmetric about the mean of the data. For a perfectly symmetric normal curve, the median and the mean are the same. The data that fit a normal curve are distributed as follows:

- Approximately 68% of the data lies within 1 standard deviation of the mean (between $\bar{x} - s$ and $\bar{x} + s$).
- Approximately 95% of the data lies within 2 standard deviations of the mean (between $\bar{x} - 2s$ and between $\bar{x} + 2s$).
- Approximately 99.7% of the data lies within 2 standard deviations of the mean (between $\bar{x} - 3s$ and between $\bar{x} + 3s$).

The shape of the curve varies somewhat based on the magnitude of the standard deviation. If the deviation is small, the curve will be horizontally compressed and will be tall and thin. If the deviation is large, the curve will be horizontally stretched and will appear flatter.

The area under the normal curve is 1. The probability of any given interval can be found by calculating the area under the curve over that interval. A graphing calculator may be used to calculate areas on intervals.

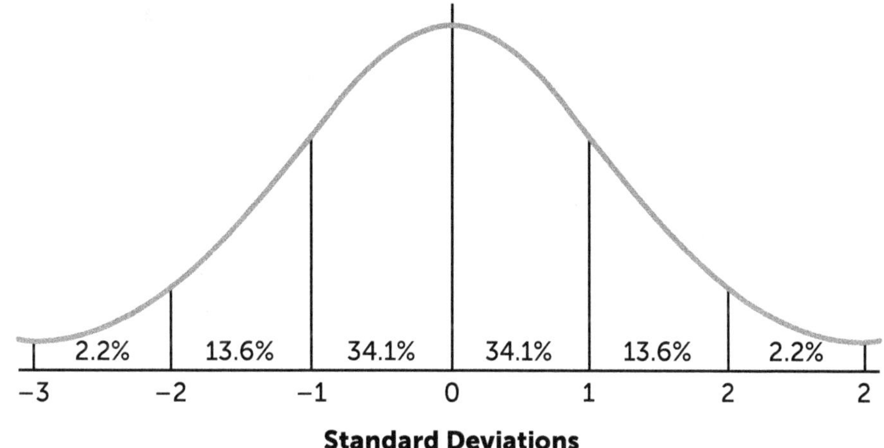

Figure 5.12. Normal Distribution

EXAMPLE

16. A common example of a normal curve distribution is the IQ test, as shown below. What is the probability that a person chosen at random has an IQ lower than 130?

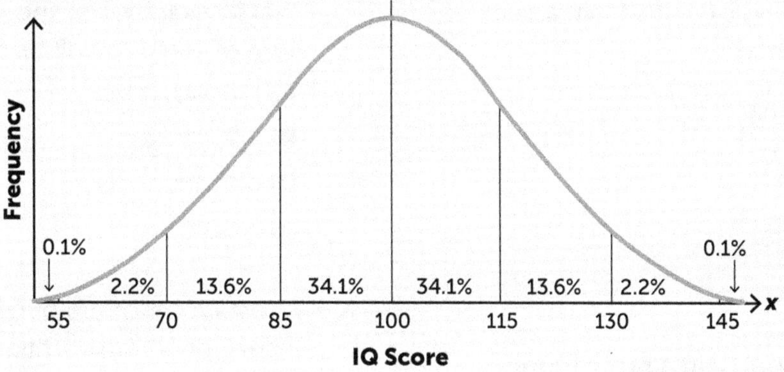

Test Your Knowledge

Work the problem, and then choose the most correct answer.

1. Robbie has a bag of treats that contains 5 pieces of gum, 7 pieces of taffy, and 8 pieces of chocolate. If Robbie reaches into the bag and randomly pulls out a treat, what is the probability that Robbie will get a piece of taffy?

   A) $\frac{1}{7}$

   B) $\frac{7}{20}$

   C) $\frac{7}{13}$

   D) $\frac{13}{20}$

2. What is the probability of selecting either a king of spades or a king of clubs from a deck of 52 cards?

   A) $\frac{1}{104}$

   B) $\frac{1}{52}$

   C) $\frac{1}{26}$

   D) $\frac{3}{52}$

3. A school held a raffle to raise money. If a person who bought 3 tickets had a 0.0004 chance of winning, what is the total number of tickets sold for the raffle?

   A) 2,400 tickets

   B) 3,500 tickets

   C) 5,000 tickets

   D) 7,500 tickets

4. The mean of 13 numbers is 30. The mean of 8 of these numbers is 42. What is the mean of the other 5 numbers? Write in the answer:

   ____

5. A bag contains 6 blue, 8 silver, and 4 green marbles. Two marbles are drawn from the bag. What is the probability that the second marble drawn will be green if replacement is not allowed?

   A) $\frac{2}{9}$

   B) $\frac{4}{17}$

   C) $\frac{11}{17}$

   D) $\frac{7}{9}$

6. A pair of 6-sided dice is rolled 10 times. What is the probability that in exactly 3 of those rolls, the sum of the dice will be 5?

   A) 0.14%

   B) 7.2%

   C) 11.1%

   D) 60%

7. A restaurant offers burritos on a corn or a flour tortilla, 5 types of meat, 6 types of cheese, and 3 different toppings. When ordering, customers can choose 1 type of tortilla, 1 meat, and 1 cheese. They can then add any of the 3 toppings. How many different burrito combinations are possible? Write in the answer:

   ____

8. How many unique ways can the letters in the word *FOGGIER* be arranged? Write in the answer:

   ____

Answer Key

EXAMPLES

1. Begin by making a table with columns for p, q, $\sim p$, and $\sim q$. Then create and fill in columns for the left statement and the right statement.

p	q	$\sim p$	$\sim q$	$p \vee q$	$\sim(p \vee q)$	$\sim p \wedge \sim q$
T	T	F	F	T	F	F
T	F	F	T	T	F	F
F	T	T	F	T	F	F
F	F	T	T	F	T	T

The last two columns have the exact same truth values, which means the statements are logically equivalent. Thus, **the proposition is a true statement.**

2. A. $\overline{A}$ includes all elements of the universal set that are not in set A:

$\overline{A}$ = **{−9, −8, −7, −6, −4, −3, −2, −1, 1, 2, 3, 4, 6, 7, 8, 9}**.

B. $A \cup B$ is all elements in either A or B:

$A \cup B$= **{ −10, −5, 0, 5, 10, −8, −6, −4, −2, 2, 4, 6, 8}**

C. $A \cap B$ is all elements in both A and B:

$A \cap B$= **{−10, 0, 10}**

D. $\overline{A} \cap \overline{B}$ is all the elements of the universal set that are not in either A or B:

$\overline{A} \cap \overline{B}$ = **{−9, −7, −3, −1, 1, 3, 7, 9}**

3.

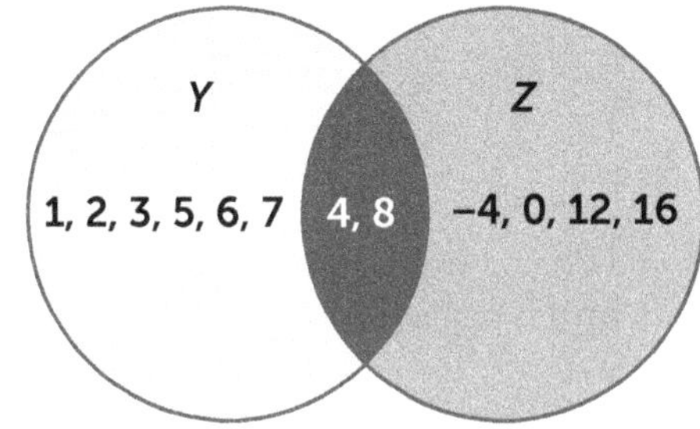

4. Multiply the number of outcomes for each individual event:

(70)(2)(5) = **700 outfits**

5. The order of the items doesn't matter, so use the formula for combinations:

$$C(n,r) = \frac{n!}{(n-r)!r!}$$

$$C(20,3) = \frac{20!}{(20-3)!3!}$$

$$= \frac{20!}{(17!\,3!)} = \frac{(20)(19)(18)}{3!}$$

= **1140 possible teams**

6. To find the number of unique permutations of 5 letters in pickle, use the permutation formula:

$P(n,r) = \frac{n!}{(n-r)!}$

$P(6,5) = \frac{6!}{(6-5)!} = \frac{720}{1} = \mathbf{720}$

7. The letter *e* repeats 3 times in the word *cheese*, meaning some permutations of the 6 letters will be indistinguishable from others. The number of permutations must be divided by the number of ways the three e's can be arranged to account for these redundant outcomes:

total number of permutations

$= \frac{\text{number of ways of arranging 6 letters}}{\text{number of ways of arranging 3 letters}}$

$= \frac{6!}{3!} = 6 \times 5 \times 4 = \mathbf{120}$

8. $P(\text{rolling even}) = \frac{\text{number of favorable outcomes}}{\text{total number of possible outcomes}} = \frac{3}{6} = \mathbf{\frac{1}{2}}$

$P(\text{rolling 5}) = \frac{\text{number of favorable outcomes}}{\text{total number of possible outcomes}} = \mathbf{\frac{1}{6}}$

9. $P(\text{not winning}) = \frac{\text{number of favorable outcomes}}{\text{total number of possible outcomes}} = \frac{14}{20} = \frac{7}{10}$ or

$P(\text{not winning}) = 1 - P(\text{winning}) = 1 - \frac{6}{20} = \frac{14}{20} = \mathbf{\frac{7}{10}}$

10. $\text{P} = \frac{\text{number of favorable outcomes}}{\text{total number of possible outcomes}} = \frac{\text{number of 3-consonant combinations}}{\text{number of 3-tile combinations}} = \frac{{}_{21}C_3}{{}_{26}C_3}$

$= \frac{1330}{2600} = 0.51 = \mathbf{51\%}$

11. This is a union (*or*) problem.

$P(A)$ = the probability of drawing a queen = $\frac{1}{13}$

$P(B)$ = the probability of drawing a heart = $\frac{1}{4}$

$P(A \cap B)$ = the probability of drawing a heart and a queen = $\frac{1}{52}$

$P(A \cup B) = P(A) + P(B) - P(A \cap B)$

$= \frac{1}{13} + \frac{1}{4} - \frac{1}{52}$

$= \mathbf{0.31}$

12. This scenario includes two events, *A* and *B*.

The probability of the first person drawing a long straw is an independent event:

$P(A) = \frac{28}{30}$

The probability the second person draws a long straw changes because one long straw has already been drawn. In other words, it is the probability of event *B* given that event *A* has already happened:

$P(B|A) = \frac{27}{29}$

The conditional probability formula can be used to determine the probability of both people drawing long straws:

$P(A \cap B) = P(A)P(B|A)$

$= \left(\frac{28}{30}\right)\left(\frac{27}{29}\right)$

$= 0.87$

There is an **87% chance** that neither of the first two individuals will draw short straws.

13. Identify the variables given in the problem.

$p = \frac{1}{6}$

$q = \frac{5}{6}$

$n = 10$

$r = 4$

Plug these values into the binomial probability formula.

$P = {}_nC_r(p^r)(q^{n-r})$

$= \left(\frac{10!}{(10-4)!4!}\right)\left(\frac{1}{6}\right)^4\left(\frac{5}{6}\right)^{10-4}$

$= 0.054$

There is a **5.4% chance**.

14. Let X be a random variable that represents the sum of two balls. The possible values of X are 3, 4, 5, 6, 7, 8, 9, 10, and 11.

There are ${}_6C_2 = \frac{6!}{4!2!} = 15$ ways to choose two ball:

	1	2	3	4	5	6
1						
2	3					
3	4	5				
4	5	6	7			
5	6	7	8	9		
6	7	8	9	10	11	

The frequency of each X value can be found by counting how many times it appears in the table. The probability of each X value will then be the frequency divided by the total number of outcomes (15).

***X* (sum)**	**Frequency**	***P*(*X*)**
3	1	$\frac{1}{15}$
4	1	$\frac{1}{15}$
5	2	$\frac{2}{15}$
6	2	$\frac{2}{15}$

X (sum)	Frequency	$P(X)$
7	3	$\frac{1}{5}$
8	2	$\frac{2}{15}$
9	2	$\frac{2}{15}$
10	1	$\frac{1}{15}$
11	1	$\frac{1}{15}$

To find the number of times 3 would appear in 50 trials, use the expected value equation with the single probability:

$\mu = np$

$50\left(\frac{1}{15}\right) = 3.33$ times

To find the average value, use the expected value equation:

$E(X) = \sum_{(i=1)}^{9} x_i P(x_i) = 3\left(\frac{1}{15}\right) + 4\left(\frac{1}{15}\right) + 5\left(\frac{2}{15}\right) + \ldots + 11\left(\frac{1}{15}\right) = \mathbf{7}$

15. Begin by defining random variable X, which represents the amount of time of a delay. Organize the data into intervals:

Delay times X:	$0 < X \leq 20$	$20 < X \leq 40$	$40 < X \leq 60$	$60 < X \leq 80$	$80 < X \leq 100$
$P(a < X \leq b)$:	0.269	0.423	0.115	0.077	0.115

The probability the delay is less than 40 minutes is:

$P(0 < X \leq 20 \text{ or } 20 < X \leq 40) = 0.26 + 0.423 = \mathbf{0.692}$

16. The probability that a person chosen at random has an IQ lower than 130 is 1 – P(IQ is above 130)

= 1 – (0.022 + 0.001) = **0.977, or 97.7%**

TEST YOUR KNOWLEDGE

1. **B) is correct.** Use the equation for probability.

$$\text{probability} = \frac{\text{possible favorable outcomes}}{\text{all possible outcomes}}$$

$$= \frac{7}{(5+7+8)} = 20$$

$$= \mathbf{\frac{7}{20}}$$

2. **C) is correct.** Use the formula for probability.

$$\text{probability} = \frac{\text{desired outcomes}}{\text{possible outcomes}}$$

$$= \frac{2 \text{ cards}}{52 \text{ cards}} = \mathbf{\frac{1}{26}}$$

3. **D) is correct.** Rearrange the formula for probability to solve for the number of possible outcomes.

$$\text{probability} = \frac{\text{desired outcomes}}{\text{possible outcomes}}$$

$$\text{possible outcomes} = \frac{\text{desired outcomes}}{\text{probability}}$$

$$= \frac{3}{0.0004} = \mathbf{7{,}500 \text{ tickets}}$$

4. **10.8 is correct.** Find the sum of the 13 numbers whose mean is 30.

$13 \times 30 = 390$

Find the sum of the 8 numbers whose mean is 42.

$8 \times 42 = 336$

Find the sum and mean of the remaining 5 numbers.

$390 - 336 = 54$

$\frac{54}{5} = 10.8$

5. **A) is correct.** Find the probability that the second marble will be green if the first marble is blue, silver, or green, and then add these probabilities together.

$P(\text{first blue and second green}) = P(\text{blue}) \times P(\text{green}|\text{first blue}) =$

$\frac{6}{18} \times \frac{4}{17} = \frac{4}{51}$

$P(\text{first silver and second green}) = P(\text{silver}) \times P(\text{green}|\text{first silver}) =$

$\frac{8}{18} \times \frac{4}{17} = \frac{16}{153}$

$P(\text{first green and second green}) = P(\text{green}) \times P(\text{green}|\text{first green}) =$

$\frac{4}{18} \times \frac{3}{17} = \frac{2}{51}$

$P(\text{second green}) = \frac{4}{51} + \frac{16}{153} + \frac{2}{51} = \mathbf{\frac{2}{9}}$

6. **B) is correct.** Use the equation for Bernoulli trials (binomial distribution).

$P = {}_nC_r(p^r)(q^{n-r})$

$n = 10$

$r = 3$

$p = \frac{4}{36} = \frac{1}{9}$

$q = \frac{8}{9}$

$P = {}_{10}C_3\left(\frac{1}{9}\right)^3\left(\frac{8}{9}\right)^7 = 0.072 =$ **7.2%**

7. **480 is correct.** Use the fundamental counting principle. Each topping has two possible choices (yes or no).

   2(5)(6)(2)(2)(2) = 480

8. **2520 is correct.** Use the fundamental counting principle to find the number of ways the letters can be arranged. Because the two *G*'s are indistinguishable, divide by the number of ways those 2 letters can be arranged.

   $\frac{7!}{2!} = (7)(6)(5)(4)(3) = 2520$

CHAPTER SIX
Practice Test

Work the problem, and then choose the most correct answer.

1. To which of the following number sets does 3 not belong?

A) irrational

B) rational

C) whole

D) integer

2. Which of the following is a solution of the given equation?

$4(m + 4)^2 - 4m^2 + 20 = 276$

A) 3

B) 6

C) 12

D) 24

3. Which of the following is the *y*-intercept of the given equation?

$7y - 42x + 7 = 0$

A) $(0, \frac{1}{6})$

B) (6,0)

C) (0,–1)

D) (–1,0)

4. A restaurant offers burritos on a corn or a flour tortilla, 5 types of meat, 6 types of cheese, and 3 different toppings. When ordering, customers can choose 1 type of tortilla, 1 meat, and 1 cheese. They can then add any of the 3 toppings. How many different burrito combinations are possible?

____

5. A cube is inscribed in a sphere such that each vertex on the cube touches the sphere. If the volume of the sphere is 972π cm^3, what is the approximate volume of the cube in cubic centimeters?

A) 9

B) 10.4

C) 1125

D) 1729

6. If a student answers 42 out of 48 questions correctly on a quiz, what percentage of questions did she answer correctly?

   A) 82.5%

   B) 85%

   C) 87.5%

   D) 90%

7. Which inequality is represented by the following graph?

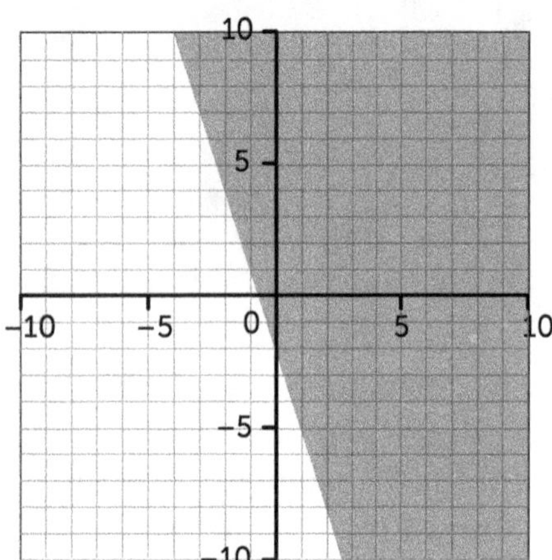

   A) $y \geq -3x - 2$

   B) $y \geq 3x - 2$

   C) $y > -3x - 2$

   D) $y \leq -3x - 2$

8. The inequality $6 > x^2 - x$ is true for which of the following values of x?

   I. $x < -2$

   II. $-2 < x < -3$

   III. $x > 3$

   A) I only

   B) II only

   C) III only

   D) I and III only

9. Simplify: $\frac{7.2 \times 10^6}{1.6 \times 10^{-3}}$

   A) 4.5×10^{-9}

   B) 4.5×10^{-3}

   C) 4.5×10^{3}

   D) 4.5×10^{9}

10. How many unique ways can the letters in the word *FOGGIER* be arranged?

   A) 42

   B) 1050

   C) 2520

   D) 5040

11. Rectangular water tank A is 5 feet long, 10 feet wide, and 4 feet tall. Rectangular tank B is 5 feet long, 5 feet wide, and 4 feet tall. If the same amount of water is poured into both tanks and the height of the water in Tank A is 1 foot, how high will the water be in Tank B?

____

12. What is the value of z in the following system?

   $z - 2x = 14$

   $2z - 6x = 18$

____

13. Which expression is equivalent to dividing 300 by 12?

   A) 2(150 – 6)

   B) (300 ÷ 4) ÷ 6

   C) (120 ÷ 6) + (180 ÷ 6)

   D) (120 ÷ 12) + (180 ÷ 12)

14. Using the information in the table, which equation demonstrates the linear relationship between x and y?

x	y
3	3
7	15
10	24

   A) $y = 6x - 6$

   B) $y = 5x - 6$

   C) $y = 4x - 6$

   D) $y = 3x - 6$

15. The pie graph below shows how a state's government plans to spend its annual budget of \$3 billion. How much more money does the state plan to spend on infrastructure than education?

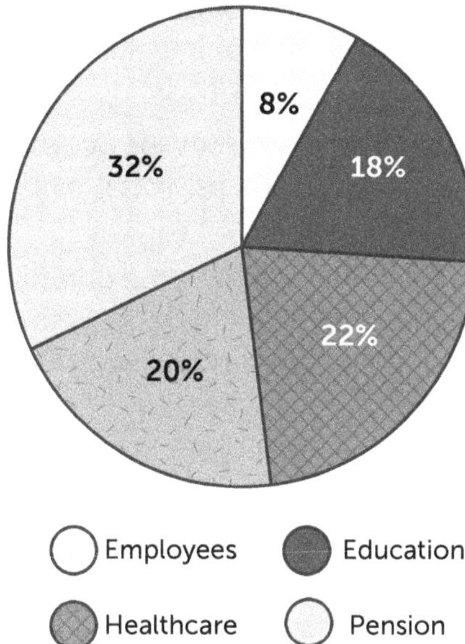

A) \$60,000,000

B) \$120,000,000

C) \$300,000,000

D) \$600,000,000

16. If $\Delta ABD \sim \Delta DEF$ and the similarity ratio is 3:4, what is the measure of *DE* if *AB* = 12?

____

17. The number of chairs in the front row of a movie theater is 14. Each subsequent row contains 2 more seats than the row in front of it. If the theater has 25 rows, what is the total number of seats in the theater?

A) 336

B) 350

C) 888

D) 950

18. Solve for *x*:

$x = 6(3^0)$

A) 0

B) 6

C) 18

D) 180

19. In the fall, 425 students pass the math benchmark. In the spring, 680 students pass the same benchmark. What is the percentage increase in passing scores from fall to spring?

A) 37.5%

B) 55%

C) 60%

D) 62.5%

20. Bryce has 34 coins worth a total of \$6.25. If all the coins are dimes or quarters, how many of each coin does he have?

A) 9 dimes and 15 quarters

B) 10 dimes and 24 quarters

C) 15 dimes and 19 quarters

D) 19 dimes and 15 quarters

21. A pair of 6-sided dice is rolled 10 times. What is the probability that in exactly 3 of those rolls, the sum of the dice will be 5?

A) 0.14%

B) 7.2%

C) 11.1%

D) 60%

22. A person earning a salary between \$75,000 and \$100,000 per year will pay \$10,620 in taxes plus 20% of any amount over \$75,000. What would a person earning \$80,000 per year pay in taxes?

____

23. Which of the following defines y as a function of x?

I. $y^2 + x = 3$

II.

x	y
0	4
1	5
2	8
3	13
4	20

III.

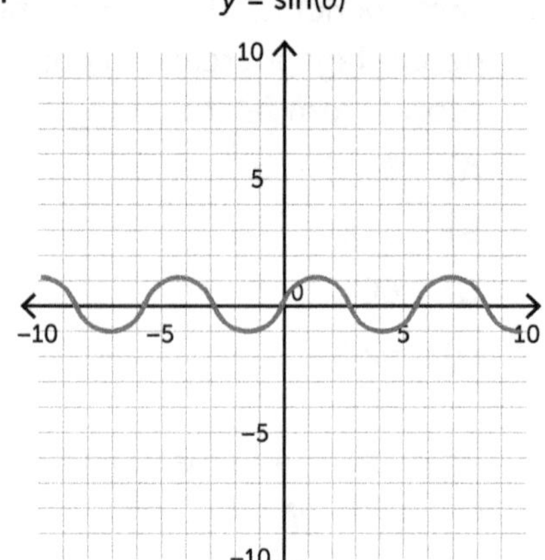

A) II only

B) I and II only

C) II and III only

D) I, II, III only

24. What is the solution set for the inequality $2x^2 - 4x - 6 < 0$?

A) $(-1,3)$

B) $(-\infty,\infty)$

C) $\varnothing$

D) $(-\infty,-1) \cup (3,\infty)$

25. If $y = 2x^2 + 12x - 3$ is written if the form $y = a(x - h)^2 + k$, what is the value of k?

A. –3

B. –15

C. –18

D. –21

26. What transformation is created by the –3 in the graph of $y = -3|x - 2| + 2$?

A) The –3 moves the vertex down 3 and reflects the graph over the x-axis.

B) The –3 moves the vertex to the left 3 and widens the graph.

C) The –3 makes the graph wider and reflects it over the x-axis.

D) The –3 makes the graph narrower and reflects the graph over the x-axis.

27. Juan plans to spend 25% of his workday writing a report. If he is at work for 9 hours, how many hours will he spend writing the report?

A) 2.25

B) 2.50

C) 2.75

D) 4.00

28. What is the total number of 6-digit numbers in which each individual digit is less than 3 or greater than 6?

A) 38,880

B) 46,656

C) 80,452

D) 101,370

29. If $\Delta JKL \sim \Delta PQR$ and $JK = 10$, $KL = 18.2$, $JL = 13.4$, and $QR = 47.1$, what is the approximate perimeter of ΔPQR?

A) 42

B) 80

C) 108

D) 135

30. Which conclusion can be drawn from the graph?

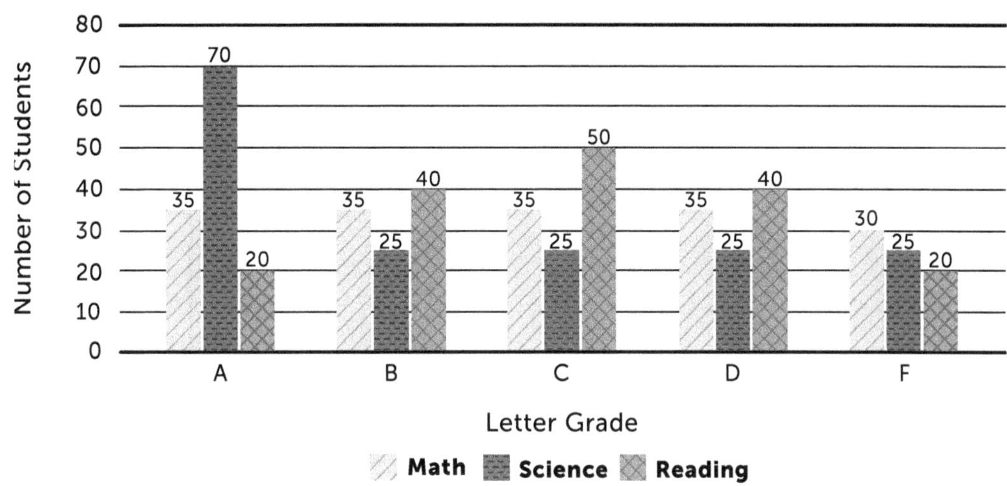

A. More than twice as many students earned an A in science than earned an F in science.

B. The majority of the students earned a C in math.

C. The number of students who earned a B in reading is equal to the number of students who earned a B in math.

D. Next year's students will not need intensive science instruction.

31. If angles *a* and *b* are congruent, what is the measurement of angle *c*?

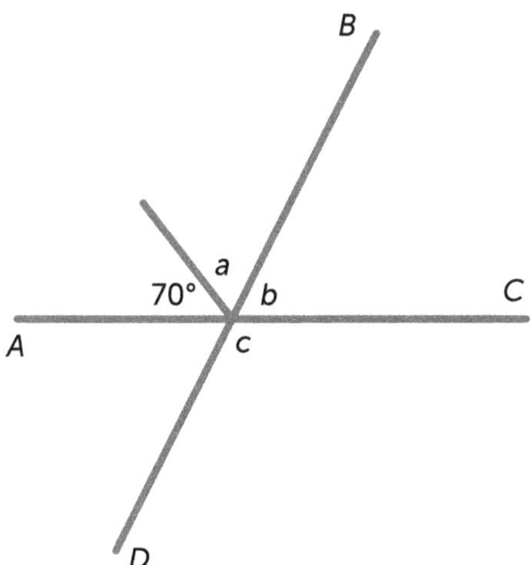

A) 70°

B) 125°

C) 110°

D) 55°

32. What is the domain of the piece-wise function shown in the graph?

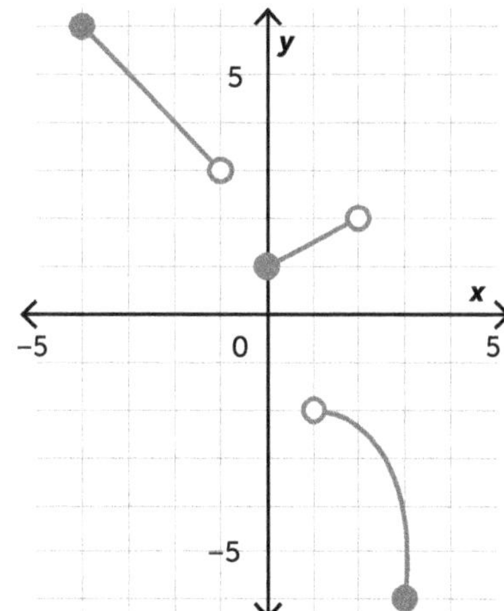

A) $D: (-4,-1) \cup (0,3)$

B) $D: (-4,3)$

C) $D: (-4,1) \cup (0,3)$

D) $D: (-4,-1) \cup (0,1) \cup (1,3)$

33. Which graph shows the solution to $y = 2x + 1$?

A)

B) 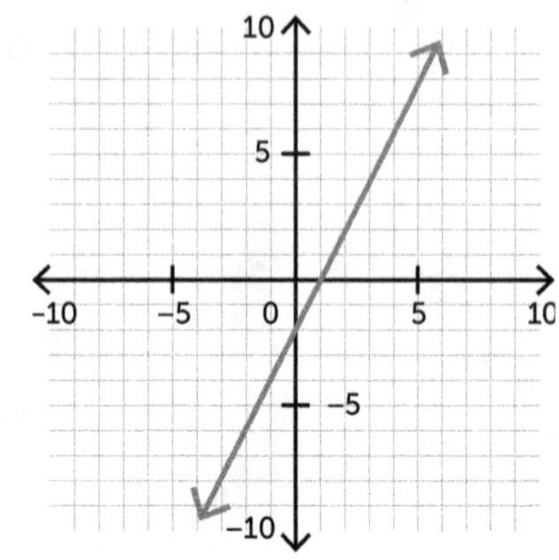

C) 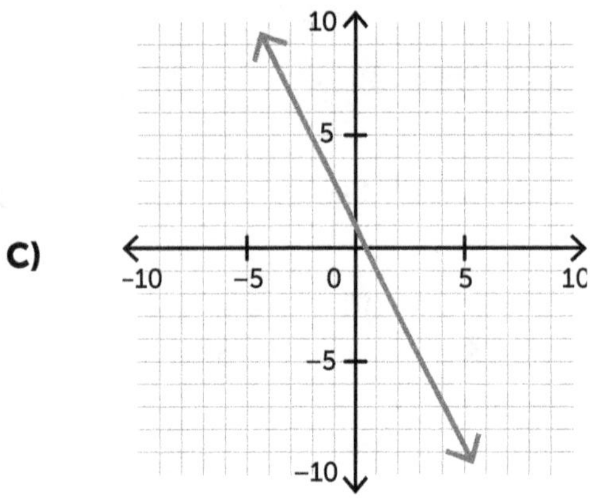

D) 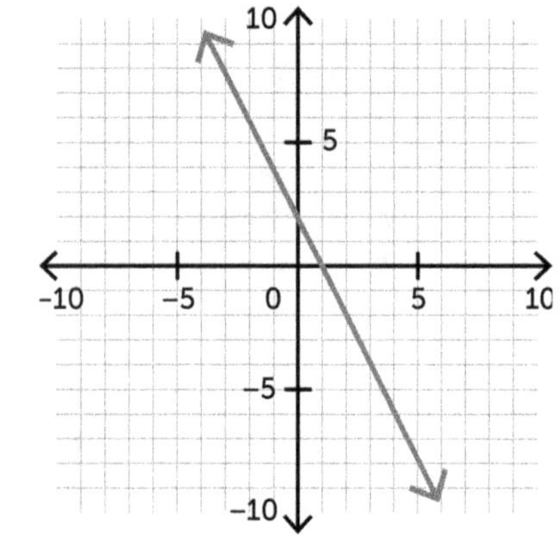

34. In a high school with 1,200 students, 200 students are in the band and 150 are in the math club. If 20 students are in both the band and the math club, how many students are in neither the band nor the math club?

____

35. A bike store is having a 30%-off sale, and one of the bikes is on sale for $385. What was the original price of this bike?

A) $253.00

B) $450.00

C) $500.50

D) $550.00

36. Which equation describes the relationship between x and y shown in the table?

x	y
−1	−1
−2	−8
−3	−27

A) $y = -x^3$

B) $y = x^3$

C) $y = x - 6$

D) $y = -x^2 + 1$

37. Find $(f - g)(x)$ if $f(x) = x^2 + 16x$ and $g(x) = 5x^2 + 4x + 25$.

A) $-4x^2 + 12x - 25$

B) $-4x^2 - 12x - 25$

C) $-4x^2 - 20x + 25$

D) $4x^2 - 20x - 25$

38. The line $f(x)$ is shown on the graph below. If $g(x) = f(x - 2) + 3$, which of the following points lies on $g(x)$?

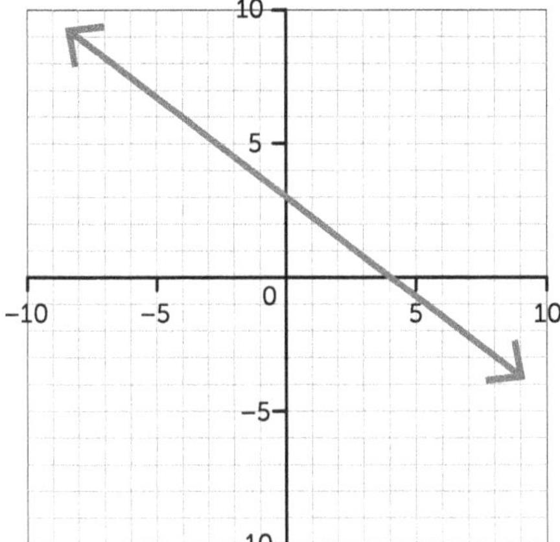

A) (1,2)

B) (2,3)

C) (6,3)

D) (7,2)

39. A data set contains information on the hours worked in a government department. Which of the following statistics would have a unit that is NOT hours?

A) variance

B) standard deviation

C) range

D) interquartile range

40. What is the domain of the inequality $\left|\frac{x}{8}\right| \geq 1$?

A) $(-\infty,\infty)$

B) $[8,\infty)$

C) $(-\infty,-8]$

D) $(-\infty,-8] \cup [8,\infty)$

41. Find the 12th term of the following sequence.

−57, −40, −23, −6...

____

42. The number of individuals, N, in a certain population of deer is expected to increase every year by 5 percent. If the current population is 14,300 individuals, which of the following best describes the size of the population in t years?

A) $N(t) = 14{,}300(0.05)^t$

B) $N(t) = 14{,}300(1.05)^t$

C) $N(t) = 14{,}300^{1.05t}$

D) $N(t) = 14{,}300^{0.5t}$

43. In the Venn diagram below, V represents the set of all vehicles, M represents the set of all motorized vehicles, and A represents the set of all automobiles.

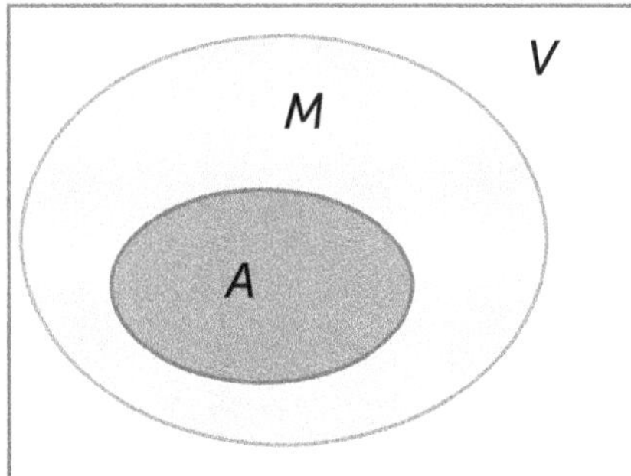

Based on the diagram, which statement is an *invalid* conclusion?

A) All motorized vehicles are vehicles.

B) Some automobiles and motorized vehicles are not vehicles.

C) All automobiles are vehicles.

D) Some vehicles are automobiles.

44. A grocery store sold 30% of its pears and had 455 pears remaining. How many pears did the grocery store start with?

____

45. Which statement about the following set is true?

{60, 5, 18, 20, 37, 37, 11, 90, 72}

A) The median and the mean are equal.

B) The mean is less than the mode.

C) The mode is greater than the median.

D) The median is less than the mean.

46. A baby weighed 7.5 pounds at birth and gained weight at a rate of 6 ounces per month for the first six months. Which equation describes the baby's weight in ounces, y, after t months?

A) $y = 6t + 7.5$

B) $y = 6t + 120$

C) $y = 7.5t + 120$

D) $y = 6t + 7.5$

47. A bag contains 6 blue, 8 silver, and 4 green marbles. Two marbles are drawn from the bag. What is the probability that the second marble drawn will be green if replacement is not allowed?

A) $\frac{2}{9}$

B) $\frac{4}{17}$

C) $\frac{11}{17}$

D) $\frac{7}{9}$

48. Which of the following is the inverse of $f(x)^{-1} = \frac{7x-2}{3}$?

A) $f(x)^{-1} = \frac{3x+2}{7}$

B) $f(x)^{-1} = \frac{7x+2}{3}$

C) $f(x)^{-1} = 7x - 6$

D) $f(x)^{-1} = \frac{7y+2}{3}$

49. A wedge from a cylindrical piece of cheese was cut as shown. If the entire wheel of cheese weighed 73 pounds before the wedge was removed, what is the approximate remaining weight of the cheese?

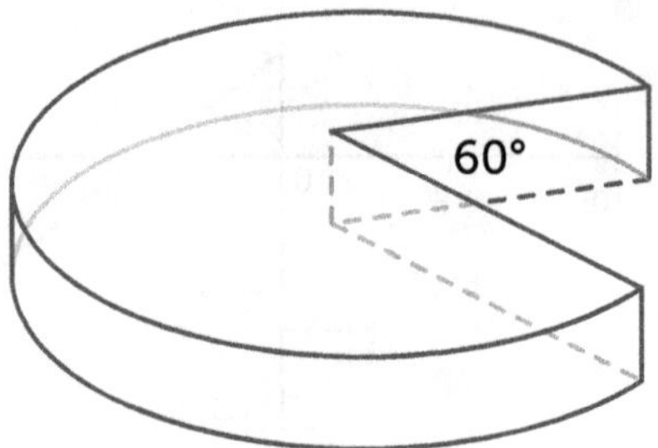

A) 12.17 pounds

B) 37.00 pounds

C) 60.83 pounds

D) 66.92 pounds

50. Kim and Chris are writing a book together. Kim wrote twice as many pages as Chris, and together they wrote 240 pages. How many pages did Chris write?

A) 80

B) 120

C) 160

D) 240

Answer Key

1. A)

The number 3 is not irrational because it can be written as the fraction $\frac{3}{1}$.

2. B)

Plug each value into the equation.

$4(3 + 4)^2 - 4(3)^2 + 20 = 180 \neq 276$

$4(6 + 4)^2 - 4(6)^2 + 20 = \mathbf{276}$

$4(12 + 4)^2 - 4(12)^2 + 20 = 468 \neq 276$

$4(24 + 4)^2 - 4(24)^2 + 20 = 852 \neq 276$

3. C)

Plug 0 in for x and solve for y.

$7y - 42x + 7 = 0$

$7y - 42(0) + 7 = 0$

$y = -1$

The y-intercept is at **(0,−1)**.

4. 480

Use the fundamental counting principle. Each topping has two possible choices (yes or no).

$2(5)(6)(2)(2)(2) = \mathbf{480}$

5. C)

Use the formula for the volume of a sphere to find its radius.

$V = \frac{4}{3}\pi r^3$

$972\pi = \frac{4}{3}\pi r^3$

$r = 9$

Use the super Pythagorean theorem to find the side of the cube.

$d^2 = a^2 + b^2 + c^2$

$18^2 = 3s^2$

$s \approx 10.4$

Use the length of the side to find the volume of the cube.

$V = s^3$

$V \approx (10.4)^3$

$V \approx \mathbf{1,125}$

6. C)

Use the formula for percentages.

$\text{percent} = \frac{\text{part}}{\text{whole}} = \frac{42}{48}$

$= 0.875 = \mathbf{87.5\%}$

7. A)

Eliminate answer choices that don't match the graph.

A) Correct.

B) The graph has a negative slope while this inequality has a positive slope.

C) The line on the graph is solid, so the inequality should include the "or equal to" symbol.

D) The shading is above the line, meaning the inequality should be "y is greater than."

8. B)

Move the terms to the same side and factor. Use the zeros to find the intervals where the inequality is true.

$6 > x^2 - x$

$0 > x^2 - x - 6$

$0 > (x + 2)(x - 3)$

For $x < -2$:

$0 \ngtr (x + 2)(x - 3)$

For $-2 < x < -3$:

$0 > (x + 2)(x - 3)$

For $x > 3$:

$\mathbf{0 \ngtr (x + 2)(x - 3)}$

9. D)

Divide the digits and subtract the exponents.

$\frac{7.2 \times 10^6}{1.6 \times 10^{-3}}$

$7.2 \div 1.6 = 4.5$

$6 - (-3) = 9$

$\mathbf{4.5 \times 10^9}$

10. C)

Use the fundamental counting principle to find the number of ways the letters can be arranged. Because the two G's are indistinguishable, divide by the number of ways those 2 letters can be arranged.

$\frac{7!}{2!} = (7)(6)(5)(4)(3) = \mathbf{2520}$

11. 2 feet

Calculate the volume of water in tank A.

$V = l \times w \times h$

$5 \times 10 \times 1 = 50 \text{ ft}^3$

Find the height this volume would reach in tank B.

$V = l \times w \times h$

$50 = 5 \times 5 \times h$

$h = \mathbf{2 \text{ ft}}$

12. 24

Solve the system using substitution.

$z - 2x = 14 \rightarrow z = 2x + 14$

$2z - 6x = 18$

$2(2x + 14) - 6x = 18$

$4x + 28 - 6x = 18$

$-2x = -10$

$x = 5$

$z - 2(5) = 14$

$\mathbf{z = 24}$

13. D)

$300 \div 12 = 25$

Test each answer choice to see if it equals 25.

A) $2(150 - 6)$

$= 2(144)$

$= 288 \neq 25$

B) $(300 \div 4) \div 6$

$= 75 \div 6$

$= 12.5 \neq 25$

C) $(120 \div 6) + (180 \div 6)$

$= 20 + 30$

$= 50 \neq 25$

D) $(120 \div 12) + (180 \div 12)$

$= (10) + (15) = 25$

14. D)

Substitute one (x,y) pair into each anser choice to find the correct equation.

A) $y = 6x - 6$; (3,3)

$y = 6(3) - 6$

$y = 18 - 6$

$y = 12 \neq 3$

B) $y = 5x - 6$; (3,3)

$y = 5(3) - 6$

$y = 15 - 6$

$y = 9 \neq 3$

C) $y = 4x - 6$; (3,3)

$y = 4(3) - 6$

$y = 12 - 6$

$y = 6 \neq 3$

D) $y = 3x - 6$; (3,3)

$y = 3(3) - 6$

$y = 9 - 6$

$\mathbf{y = 3}$

15. A)

Find the amount the state will spend on infrastructure and

education, and then find the difference.

infrastructure = 0.2(3,000,000,000) = 600,000,000

education = 0.18(3,000,000,000) = 540,000,000

600,000,000 – 540,000,000 = **$60,000,000**

16. 16

Set up a proportion and solve.

$\frac{AB}{DE} = \frac{3}{4}$

$\frac{12}{DE} = \frac{3}{4}$

$3(DE) = 48$

$\mathbf{DE = 16}$

17. D)

Use the formula for an arithmetic sum.

$S_n = \frac{n}{2}(2a_1 + (n-1)d)$

$= \frac{25}{2}(2(14) + (25-1)2) = \mathbf{950}$

18. B)

$6(3^0) = 6(1) = \mathbf{6}$

19. 60%

Use the formula for percent change.

$\text{percent change} = \frac{\text{amount of change}}{\text{original amount}}$

$= \frac{(680-425)}{425}$

$= \frac{255}{425} = 0.60 = \mathbf{60\%}$

20. C)

Set up a system of equations where *d* equals the number of dimes and *q* equals number of quarters.

$d + q = 34$

$0.1d + 0.25q = 6.25$

$0.1d + 0.25(34 - d) = 6.25$

$d = 15$

$q = 34 - 15 = \mathbf{19}$

21. B)

Use the equation for Bernoulli trials (binomial distribution).

$P = {}_nC_r\,(p^r)(q^{n-r})$

$n = 10$

$r = 3$

$p = \frac{4}{36} = \frac{1}{9}$

$q = \frac{8}{9}$

$P = {}_{10}C_3\left(\frac{1}{9}\right)^3\left(\frac{8}{9}\right)^7 = 0.072 = \mathbf{7.2\%}$

22. $11,620

Add the base amount and the tax on the extra percentage of the person's income.

10,620 + 0.2(80,000 – 75,000) = **$11,620**

23. B)

Only I and II define *y* as a function of *x*.

I. This is not a function: the equation represents a horizontal parabola, which fails the vertical line test.

II. This is a function: each *x*-value corresponds to only one *y*-value.

III. This is a function: the graph passes the vertical line test.

24. A)

Use the zeros of the function to find the intervals where it is less than 0.

$2x^2 - 4x - 6 = 0$

$(2x - 6)(x + 1) = 0$

$x = 3$ and $x = -1$

$(-\infty,-1) \rightarrow 2x^2 - 4x - 6 > 0$

$(-1,3) \rightarrow 2x^2 - 4x - 6 < 0$

$(3,\infty) \rightarrow 2x^2 - 4x - 6 > 0$

The function is less than 0 on the interval **(−1,3)**.

25. D)

Complete the square to put the quadratic equation in vertex form.

$y = 2x^2 + 12x - 3$

$y = 2(x^2 + 6x + \_\_\_\_\_) - 3 + \_\_\_\_\_$

$y = 2(x^2 + 6x + 9) - 3 - 18$

$\mathbf{y = 2(x + 3)^2 - 21}$

26. D)

For the function $y = a|x - h| + k$:

When $|a| > 1$, the graph will narrow.

When *a* is negative, the graph is reflected over the *x*-axis.

27. A)

Use the equation for percentages.

part = whole × percentage = 9 × 0.25 = **2.25**

28. A)

There are six digits that can be used to make up the 6-digit number: 0, 1, 2, 7, 8, and 9. However, 0 cannot be used for the first digit. Use the fundamental counting principle: (5)(6)(6)(6)(6)(6) = **38,880**.

29. C)

Find the perimeter of ΔJKL.

$P = 10 + 18.2 + 13.4 = 41.6$

Find the scale factor between the two triangles.

$\frac{QR}{KL} = \frac{47.1}{18.2} = 2.588$

Multiply the perimeter of ΔJKL by the scale factor to find the perimeter of ΔPQR.

$(2.588)(41.6) = 107.6 \approx \mathbf{108}$

30. A)

A. Twenty-five students earned an F in science, and 70 students earned an A in science; 2(25) < 70.

B. There are 170 total students with math grades. A majority would be more than half (85). Only 25 students earned a C in math.

C. Forty students earned a B in reading and 35 students earned a B in math.

D. The graph does not include information about next year's students.

31. B)

Use the two sets of linear angles to find *b* and then *c*.

$a = b$

$a + b + 70 = 180$

$2a + 70 = 180$

$a = b = 55°$

$b + c = 180°$ $55 + c = 180$

$c = \mathbf{125°}$

32. A)

The domain is the possible values of *x* from left to right. Here, the domain starts at −4, inclusive, and stops at −1, exclusive. It starts again at 0, inclusive, and goes to 3, inclusive. The two line segments from 0 to 3 cross over each other, so the domain includes this whole interval. Note that closed circles represent inclusion (square bracket), and open circles represent exclusions (round bracket).

33. A)

The line $y = 2x + 1$ will have a slope of 2 and *y*-intercept of 1.

The lines shown in graphs C and D have negative slopes. The line in graph B has a y-intercept of -2.

Alternatively, use a table to find some coordinates, and identify the graph that contains those coordinates.

x	y
0	1
1	3
2	5

34. 870

Let B equal the set of students in the band and C equal the set of students in the math club. Use set theory to find the number of students in either the band or the math club, then subtract this number from the total number of students in the school.

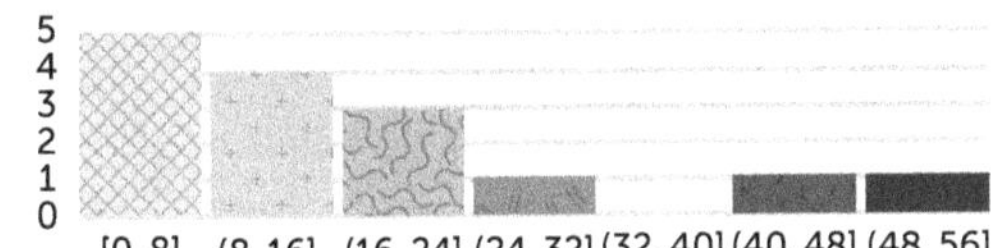

$B \cup C = B + C - B \cap C$

$= 200 + 150 - 20 = 330$

$1{,}200 - 330 = \mathbf{870}$

35. D)

Set up an equation. The original price (p) minus 30% of the original price is \$385.

$p - 0.3p = 385$

$p = \frac{385}{0.7} = \mathbf{\$550}$

36. B)

The y-value is found by cubing the x-value.

37. A)

Subtract $g(x)$ from $f(x)$.

$x^2 + 16x - (5x^2 + 4x + 25)$

$= x^2 + 16x - 5x^2 - 4x - 25$

$= \mathbf{-4x^2 + 12x - 25}$

38. C)

The function $g(x) = f(x - 2) + 3$ is a translation of $\langle 2,3 \rangle$ from $f(x)$. Test each possible point by undoing the transformation and checking if the point lies on $f(x)$.

$(1,2) \rightarrow (-1,-1)$: This point is not on $f(x)$.

$(2,3) \rightarrow (0,0)$: This point is not on $f(x)$.

$(6,3) \rightarrow (4,0)$: **This point is on $f(x)$.**

$(7,2) \rightarrow (5,-1)$: This point is not on $f(x)$.

39. A)

Variance would have a unit of hours squared, not hours.

40. D)

Split the absolute value inequality into two inequalities and simplify. Switch the inequality when making one side negative.

$\frac{x}{8} \geq 1$

$x \geq 8$

$-\frac{x}{8} \geq 1$

$\frac{x}{8} \leq -1$

$x \leq -8$

$x \leq -8$ or $x \geq 8$ ¨ $\mathbf{(-\infty,-8] \cup [8,\infty)}$

41. 130

Use the equation to find the nth term of an arithmetic sequence.

$a_1 = -57$

$d = -40 - (-57) = 17$

$n = 12$

$a_n = a_1 + d(n - 1)$

$a_{12} = -57 + 17(12 - 1)$

$\mathbf{a_{12} = 130}$

42. B)

The population is growing exponentially, so plug the values into the equation for exponential growth.

$A(t) = a(1 + r)^t$

$N(t) = 14{,}300(1 + 0.05)^t$

$\mathbf{N(t) = 14{,}300(1.05)^t}$

43. B)

Both ***A*** and ***M*** are subsets of ***V***, so *all* elements of ***A*** and ***M*** must be vehicles.

44. Set up an equation. If p is the original number of pears, the store has sold $0.30p$ pears. The original number minus the number sold will equal 455.

$p - 0.30p = 455$

$p = \frac{455}{0.7}$ = **650 pears**

45. D)

{5, 11, 18, 20, **37**, 37, 60, 72, 90}

median = 37

mode = 37

mean

$= \frac{60 + 5 + 18 + 20 + 37 + 37 + 11 + 90 + 72}{9}$

= 38.89

The median is less than the mean.

46. B)

There are 16 ounces in a pound, so the baby's starting weight is 120 ounces. He gained 6 ounces per month, or $6t$. So, the baby's weight will be his initial weight plus the amount gained for each month: $\mathbf{y = 6t + 120}$.

47. A)

Find the probability that the second marble will be green if the first marble is blue, silver, or green, and then add these probabilities together.

P(first blue and second green) = P(blue) × P(green|first blue)

$= \frac{6}{18} \times \frac{4}{17} = \frac{4}{51}$

P(first silver and second green) = P(silver) × P(green|first silver)

$= \frac{8}{18} \times \frac{4}{17} = \frac{16}{153}$

P(first green and second green) = P(green) × P(green|first green)

$= \frac{4}{18} \times \frac{3}{17} = \frac{2}{51}$

P(second green) = $\frac{4}{51} + \frac{16}{153} + \frac{2}{51}$

$= \mathbf{\frac{2}{9}}$

48. A)

Replace $f(x)$ with y, then swap x and y in the equation and solve for y.

$y = \frac{7x - 2}{3}$

$x = \frac{7y - 2}{3}$

$3x = 7y - 2$

$3x + 2 = 7y$

$\frac{3x + 2}{7} = y$

$\mathbf{f(x) = \frac{3x + 2}{7}}$

49. C)

Set up a proportion to find the weight of the removed wedge.

$\frac{60°}{x \text{ lb.}} = \frac{360°}{73 \text{ lb.}}$

$x \approx 12.17$ lb.

Subtract the removed wedge from the whole to find the weight of the remaining piece.

73 – 12.17 = **60.83**

50. A)

p = # of pages written by Chris

$2p$ = # of pages written by Kim

$p + 2p = 240$

$p = 80$

Follow the link below to take your second CLEP College Mathematics practice test and to access other online study resources:

http://www.acceptedinc.com/clep-college-math-online-resources

Printed in the USA
CPSIA information can be obtained
at www.ICGtesting.com
LVHW010208131023
760673LV00061B/1215

9 781635 309744